New Orleans
Orleans
⇛· in the ·⇚
TWENTIES

The Tchoupitoulas Streetcar at the corner of Race and Tchoupitoulas streets, March 1925. Two men operated the streetcar, a motorman and a conductor. The motorman is wearing a white dress shirt and tie. (Photo by Charles L. Franck, courtesy Ken and Lynn Cheskin for the late Abe Oppenheim)

New Orleans
⫸ in the ⫷
TWENTIES

Mary Lou Widmer

Foreword by
Samuel Wilson, Jr., F.A.I.A.

Pelican Publishing Company
GRETNA 1993

The word "Pelican" and the depiction of a pelican are
trademarks of Pelican Publishing Company, Inc., and are
registered in the U.S. Patent and Trademark Office.

Library of Congress Cataloging-in-Publication Data

Widmer, Mary Lou, 1926-
    New Orleans in the twenties / Mary Lou Widmer ; foreword by Samuel Wilson, Jr.
       p. cm.
    Includes index.
    ISBN 0-88289-933-3
    1. New Orleans (La.)—History. 2. New Orleans (La.)—Social life and customs. I. Agent
Title.
F379.N557W53 1993
976.3'35—dc20
                                                       93-13988
                                                        CIP

Manufactured in the United States of America

Published by Pelican Publishing Company, Inc.
1101 Monroe Street, Gretna, Louisiana 70053

This book is lovingly dedicated to the beautiful, bewitching, beguiling city of New Orleans, for its religion, its decadence, its food, its music, and the colorful cast of characters who gave it life in the twenties—and in every other decade.

Chartres Street in the French Quarter, and the St. Louis Cathedral, on the site of the first church in the Mississippi Valley.

Contents

Canal and North Rampart St., New Orleans, La.—113

Southern Railway Depot.   La Salle Hotel.

The Southern Railway Terminal (gray stone arch on right) was on Canal and Basin streets, facing Elks Place in the twenties. It was flanked by Krauss Department Store on the lake side and the Hotel La Salle on the river side. (The Saenger Theatre would replace the Hotel La Salle in 1927.)

Foreword

THE MEMORIES OF THE TWENTIES are retained and cherished by an ever diminishing number of New Orleanians. This was a decade of unprecedented prosperity and urban growth following the end of World War I. More and more automobiles were crowding the streets. New and taller buildings were being erected in the Central Business District. Banks were building bigger and more impressive headquarters—the Hibernia Bank Building with its temple top was to be the tallest building in the city for the next several decades. Banking rooms with great marble columns and coffered ceilings provided impressive settings for business. New hotels were being built—the Jung on Canal Street, the Bienville and the Pontchartrain on St. Charles Avenue, and annexes for the Monteleone and the Roosevelt. Office buildings like the Union Indemnity and the Pere Marquette replaced earlier structures. The use of pile foundations made all these great buildings possible. It was the driving of piles for the Pere Marquette that caused fear for the safety of the adjacent Jesuit Church, which was demolished and rebuilt on a new pile foundation.

The activities of the New Orleans Cotton Exchange so increased as to require a new building, with its old home being demolished and the sculptured ladies that ornamented its facade being erected in City Park. These seminude, voluptuous maidens were later removed, but City Park, like other New Orleans recreational facilities, continued to grow and improve. The New Orleans Country Club, after a disastrous fire, was rebuilt in 1921-22 along the New Basin Canal, which was still an active waterway from Lake Pontchartrain to Julia Street.

This was a decade of great technical progress, with the development of radio and the establishment of stations WSMB (the Saenger-Maison Blanche station) and WDSU (the DeSoto-Uhalt station). Aviation began to come into its own, culminating in the spectacular solo flight of Charles A. Lindbergh to Paris in 1927. Railroads were thriving. Rail lines connected New Orleans with all parts of the country and several stations were later consolidated into one Union Station. Streetcar lines ran on many of the city streets, and one could travel throughout the city for a fare of six cents.

NEW ORLEANS
IN THE TWENTIES

Theaters had vaudeville shows as well as moving pictures. Talking pictures came in and new and more spectacular theaters were erected. The Saenger, a "Florentine palace of splendor," Loew's State, and the Orpheum were the great entertainment centers. A torrential rain on Good Friday 1927 practically flooded the city. The theaters were inundated and hastily pumped out to open for Easter Sunday crowds, whose Easter finery was ruined by the water that had not fully dried out of the seats. Even the river threatened to overflow its banks until the levee was cut below the city in Plaquemines Parish to relieve the pressure of the high water. It was this flood that finally resulted in the construction of the Bonnet Carré Spillway to protect the city.

The 1920s were a decade of great prosperity and great speculation—a marvelous time that promised to go on forever. But the end of the decade brought an end to that golden dream. The stock market crash of 1929 suddenly changed everything. Banks closed, businesses failed, and the decade ended in an unbelievable depression.

Life went on in New Orleans and in the rest of the country, but it would be many years before the city would see the prosperity it had enjoyed before that financial disaster. This is the decade that is so vividly brought to life in this volume, the first that the author did not personally experience, but has nevertheless recreated in a fascinating way.

SAMUEL WILSON, JR., F.A.I.A.

Preface

As a writer of historical fiction and nonfiction set in New Orleans, I often wish I could go down the rabbit hole like Alice and come out in some past Wonderland, like the twenties—emerging a young woman, dressed to the nines, in cloche hat, drop-waisted frock, and long pearls—just to take a look around. Oh, what the heck, let's go!

It's a Sunday afternoon and I'm riding with friends in a Model-T Ford along the Old Shell Road to West End Park. The New Basin Canal is on our right and banks of pink oleanders blossom on our left. At West End, we take the Susquehanna Steamship across the lake to Mandeville, letting the breezes ruffle our hair as we dance to the toe-tappin' music of the Original Dixieland Jazz Band.

Back at West End, we disembark to have dinner at Mannessier's, hear the band concert, and walk over to see the fountain shooting its varicolored jets of water high into the night.

On the way home, we stop at the Holland House on City Park Avenue—oh, no, they called it Metairie Road in those days—for "a cup of coffee." Prohibition is the law of the land, but no one bothers much about it at Holland House. They serve the best Manhattan cocktails in town, and even the ladies boldly drink in nightclubs now, sipping their cocktails from thick white coffee mugs. Oh, the decadence of youth!

Afterwards, we ride through the new Pizatti Gate into City Park. The arched wrought-iron span over the entryway showcases the letters CITY PARK, illuminated by dozens of lights. We drive along palm-lined Anseman Avenue and giggle when we pass the voluptuous, seminude statues at the head of the avenue.

We exit the park on Bayou St. John, where boathouses, house boats, and squatters' shacks offer a picturesque if shabby scene. Jurisdiction over the waterway is being hotly contested in the courts and meanwhile, no one can chase the boats away. Kerosene lights burn in the little boats, and we hear soft voices calling from boat to boat.

Our day is innocent enough, but we all know that it is a decade of rebellion, a daring, scandal-loving, fad-mad time. We play mah-jongg in our Chinese kimonos, do crossword puzzles till we're cross-eyed, and chill to the newsreels of Ku

Klux Klansmen marching down Pennsylvania Avenue. We see marathon dances, Charleston contests, and aviation exhibitions. A few of us take rides in the open-air cockpits of barnstorming flyers and laugh at the barker's eerie promise, "Your money back if you get killed." Lindbergh visits New Orleans, and so does Rudolph Valentino and William Jennings Bryan.

We read F. Scott Fitzgerald and wallow in his stories of youthful sophistication and passionate love. We sing "Baby Face," "Runnin' Wild," and "Sweet Georgia Brown." We pick up a new slang word every minute. We listen to jazz, play ukeleles, and our hearts skip a beat when the boys "cut in on" us at dances.

It is a time of heroes: Babe Ruth, Johnny Weissmuller, Knute Rockne, and Jack Dempsey. Lurid tabloids are the talk of the college campuses. Our hair is short, our skirts are shorter, and our girdles are out the window. Everyone is building "crystal" sets, and Art Deco is taking over architecture. The opulence of the new moving picture palaces stuns us, and we go to the show to admire the chandeliers as much as to see the movie.

City Park triples in size. Cars are the "bee's knees," and we can buy them on the installment plan. Indoor plumbing is "in" and wood stoves are "out." The Pelicans win the pennant three times in the decade, and Martin Behrman is elected mayor again.

Best of all, everyone's making money. Stocks are selling for 10 percent of margin. Prosperity is just around the corner. Time to go back up the rabbit hole. I don't want to know how it ends.

Acknowledgments

I GRATEFULLY ACKNOWLEDGE THE HELP I received from Samuel Wilson, architectural historian, who wrote my foreword and shared much information with me. I am grateful to John Burke, columnist of "Pictures from the Past" in the *Times-Picayune*, with whom I share a love of nostalgia. I thank him for information and for the loan of several delightful family pictures.

I appreciate the help of many archivists in collecting pictures: Rev. Thomas H. Clancy, S.J., provincial archivist for Loyola University Library, and Art Carpenter, archivist; D. Clive Hardy, archivist at the UNO Library, and Beatrice R. Owsley, assistant archivist; Nancy I. Burris, librarian at the Times-Picayune Publishing Company; and John T. Magill at The Historic New Orleans Collection.

I'd like to thank Pamela Arceneaux, librarian at The Historic New Orleans Collection, and Andrea Ducros and Jane Jones, librarians at the New Orleans Public Library. Thanks to William Springer, manager of Lakewood Country Club, for the history of the club.

In the sports area, I would like to thank Arthur Schott, sports historian, who gave me information and pictures, and Al Kreider, former coach at Samuel J. Peters High School, for information on high school and college football in New Orleans in the twenties.

In the music area, thanks to the Hogan Jazz Museum at Tulane University Library for pictures.

For information on old movie houses, thanks once again to Rene Brunet, Jr., theater owner and historian, and to Jack Stewart, theater historian.

I would especially like to thank Tracy Clouatre, my photographer, who so professionally copied many pictures lent to me by collectors. Thanks to Warren Sanders of Baton Rouge, who allowed me to use many historic postcards of the twenties from his impressive collection. Thanks to Donna Fricker, photographer for the Division of Historic Preservation, for the use of her beautiful pictures. Thanks to Lloyd Huber for permission to use several pictures from his father's

13

NEW ORLEANS
IN THE TWENTIES

marvelous collection. Thanks to Arthur J. O'Keefe III, his sister Nora O. Ibert, and their late mother, Eleonora O'Keefe, for pictures of the late Mayor Arthur J. O'Keefe.

Thanks to all my writer friends who lent me delightful pictures of their parents, and to old friends who were generous with their beautiful pictures.

New Orleans
Orleans
≫· in the ·≪
TWENTIES

Audubon Park in the twenties—a place to rest and talk on wooden benches in the shade of a row of oak trees.

CHAPTER ONE

The Neighborhoods

East side, west side, all around the town

IN 1924, MY MOTHER and father were married in St. Rose de Lima Church on Bayou Road. Mother wore a lace bandeau across her forehead, an ankle-length bridal gown, and painfully pointed white satin shoes. Nobody cared much what my father wore. The only picture to record the event was of my mother, taken with a box camera in the yard of her family's Esplanade Avenue home, against a backdrop of a bedspread pegged to a clothesline by my aunt. I had to do some convincing to get my mother to let me use this picture in my book. But if it doesn't scream *the twenties,* I don't know what does.

In 1927, my mother and father moved into their newly constructed duplex on Orleans Street facing the Orleans drainage canal. The house was on the uptown side of the canal, facing a narrow dirt road for local traffic only.

On the opposite side of the canal, the street was asphalt topped, later paved, still later widened when the canal was filled in, and is today one of the few wide avenues of traffic in the city that run from the river to the lake. (Orleans Avenue makes a sharp angle at City Park Avenue and continues as Orleans on one side of the neutral ground and Marconi on the other as far as Florida Avenue. Marconi continues to the lakefront, and Orleans picks up beyond the pumping station in Lakeview. But it was all called Orleans Street in 1920, and it ran to the lake.)

Author's mother, Alma Pigeon Schultis, on her wedding day, 1924. She is wearing a brow-banded veil, pointed shoes, and long gloves. Behind her is a printed bedspread pegged to a clothesline.

EARLIER EXPANSION ALONG THE NATURAL LEVEES OF THE RIVER

A brief glimpse at the expansion upriver and downriver from the Vieux Carré (the original city) in the first two centuries will explain why some areas were settled in 1920 and others were still swampland.

From the beginning, the growing population of the city expanded along the natural levees of the Mississippi River. The first suburbs were immediately adjacent to the city and were considered part of it: Faubourg St. Mary, Faubourg Marigny, and Faubourg Treme. Then, marching in a line upriver, more distant communities became incorporated as cities and, one by one, were annexed

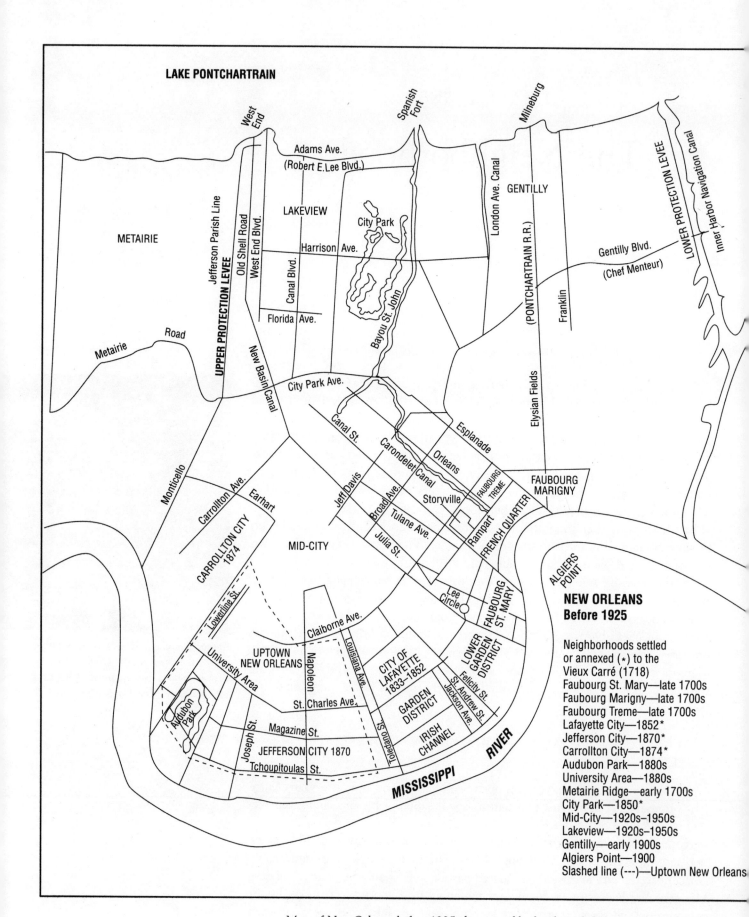

LAKE PONTCHARTRAIN

West End

Adams Ave.
(Robert E.Lee Blvd.)

Spanish Fort

Milneburg

LOWER PROTECTION LEVEE

Inner Harbor Navigation Canal

Jefferson Parish Line

Old Shell Road

West End Blvd.

LAKEVIEW

City Park

GENTILLY

London Ave. Canal

METAIRIE

UPPER PROTECTION LEVEE

Canal Blvd.

Harrison Ave.

Gentilly Blvd.
(Chef Menteur)

(PONTCHARTRAIN R.R.)

Florida Ave.

Bayou St. John

Franklin

Metairie   Road

New Basin Canal

City Park Ave.

Elysian Fields

Monticello

Canal St.

Carondelet Canal

Esplanade

Orleans

FAUBOURG TREME

FAUBOURG MARIGNY

Carrollton Ave.

Earhart

Jeff Davis

Broad Ave.

Storyville

Tulane Ave.

Rampart

FRENCH QUARTER

CARROLLTON CITY 1874

MID-CITY

Julia St.

ALGIERS POINT

Lowerline St.

Claiborne Ave.

Lee Circle

FAUBOURG ST. MARY

**NEW ORLEANS
Before 1925**

UPTOWN NEW ORLEANS

Napoleon

Louisiana Ave.

CITY OF LAFAYETTE 1833–1852

Felicity St.

St. Andrew St.

LOWER GARDEN DISTRICT

Neighborhoods settled
or annexed (∗) to the
Vieux Carré (1718)
Faubourg St. Mary—late 1700s
Faubourg Marigny—late 1700s
Faubourg Treme—late 1700s
Lafayette City—1852∗
Jefferson City—1870∗
Carrollton City—1874∗
Audubon Park—1880s
University Area—1880s
Metairie Ridge—early 1700s
City Park—1850∗
Mid-City—1920s–1950s
Lakeview—1920s–1950s
Gentilly—early 1900s
Algiers Point—1900
Slashed line (---)—Uptown New Orleans

University Area

St. Charles Ave.

GARDEN DISTRICT

Jackson Ave.

Audubon Park

Joseph St.

Magazine St.

Toledano St.

IRISH CHANNEL

RIVER

JEFFERSON CITY 1870

Tchoupitoulas St.

MISSISSIPPI

Map of New Orleans before 1925 shows neighborhoods settled or annexed to the original city
with dates. (Map by M. L. Widmer)

to New Orleans: Lafayette City, Jefferson City, and Carrollton City, in that order.

Some New Orleanians moved across the river to the West Bank, settling in the towns of Algiers and Gretna, using the excellent ferry service to take them back and forth to work in the city. But most people remained on the East Bank, where streetcar lines proliferated, offering passengers transit from considerable distances to the business district.

FAUBOURG ST. MARY

The first spillover from the original city took place in the early nineteenth century when Faubourg Marigny, downriver from the city, and Faubourg St. Mary, established in 1788 above Canal Street, were subdivided into lots.

Faubourg St. Mary had formerly been the Gravier plantation. This suburb was also called the American Sector since large numbers of Americans from the East Coast settled there after the Louisiana Purchase. Irish immigrants settled there in great numbers, after coming to New Orleans in the 1830s to dig the New Basin Canal. Testimony to this was "The Irish Channel," a nickname given to a part of the Lower Garden District. Faubourg St. Mary was bounded by Common Street, Delord (later Howard Avenue), the river, and St. Charles Avenue.

FAUBOURG MARIGNY

Faubourg Marigny, on the downtown side of the Vieux Carré, was settled by French Creoles from the Old City. This area was bounded by Esplanade, Press Street, St. Claude, and the river. It was settled by German immigrants in the early and mid-nineteenth century, and came to be called Little Saxony. Industrial activity thrived there from the beginning of the nineteenth century; Press Street was named for the cotton presses in the area.

Canal Street near St. Charles, looking toward the lake. Maison Blanche Building can be recognized by the radio tower of WSMB on the roof, upper right hand corner.

FAUBOURG TREME AND STORYVILLE

On the third side of the Vieux Carré (the river being the fourth) was Faubourg Treme, a small lakeward development adjacent to Faubourg St. Mary. The most scandalous inhabitants of this area were the "ladies of the evening" of the infamous red-light district known as Storyville (1898-1917).

During my father's boyhood, until he was seventeen (in the year 1917, when Storyville was closed down by the U.S. Navy), he had heard men talk behind their hands about the bordellos of Storyville. Accommodations in Storyville ranged in class from Lulu White's elegant Mahogany Hall to the small filthy "cribs" along Iberville Street. Daddy knew where "the district" was, as it took in a large area quite close to his neighborhood in the Vieux Carré. It was bounded by Iberville and St. Louis, Basin and Claiborne, and was a city within Faubourg Treme. There are as many different boundaries given for Faubourg Treme as there are sources, but it lay roughly between Canal and Esplanade, Rampart and Claiborne.

At Claiborne Avenue was St. Louis Cemetery No. 2. Settlement did not extend far beyond Claiborne Avenue at the turn of the century. Beyond that lay a vast expanse of swampland called "back o' town" or "the woods." Directions were given in the following fashion: "She lives at 650 Dauphine on the 'uptown woods' corner." Today we would call it the "uptown lake" corner.

Also in the Treme neighborhood was the Carondelet Canal, on which boats could travel from Basin Street (near Orleans) to Bayou St. John, and thence to Lake Pontchartrain and the Gulf Coast cities to trade. Because of the canal, a community developed from Basin Street to Claiborne Avenue. The canal was built in 1795 and filled in between the late 1920s and the late 1930s.

HOW DO I GET TO THE LAKE?

Lakeward expansion for the city's burgeoning population would not take place until twenty years and a billion dollars after the installation of the first drainage system in 1899. In the meantime, there were only two ways for people living in the city to reach the lake. One was by way of the Pontchartrain Railroad, which ran on Elysian Fields from the river to the lake, ending at the little town of Milneburg (where UNO is today). The other was by automobile on the Old Shell Road, which ran alongside the New Basin Canal from City Park Avenue to West End Park. (The Old Shell Road is today's Pontchartrain Boulevard.)

By 1920, Canal Boulevard had been cut through Cypress Grove Cemetery No. 2, a cemetery for the indigent to the east of Greenwood Cemetery. It was a narrow shell road with weeds growing on both sides, which ran from City Park Avenue to Florida Avenue, and then stopped. Motorists heading for the lake or for Spanish Fort had to turn left on Florida to West End Boulevard, then right to Robert E. Lee (Adams Avenue in the twenties) and the Turtleback Road. If Adams Avenue was not under water (which was frequently the case), that was the road to take to Spanish Fort, where Bayou St. John met the lake, a journey of another two miles.

THE GARDEN DISTRICT

New Orleans is shaped like a saucer. The "bowl" is Mid-City, which was the lowest point in this below-sea-level city. The cities along the riverfront were built along the "rim of the saucer," on natural levees built up by the river over the centuries.

The Lower Garden District is an area of primarily nineteenth-century residential and commercial development upriver from the Faubourg St. Mary and bounded approximately by Howard Avenue, Jackson Avenue, Claiborne Avenue, and the river.

The plantations adjacent to the Lower Garden District—Livaudais and Delasize—running like long ribbons of land from Magazine to St. Charles Avenue between Felicity and Toledano streets, were subdivided in 1825, and quickly became popular as a residential district for wealthy Americans (as opposed to Creoles). The area became incorporated in 1833 as Lafayette City, and was annexed to New Orleans in 1852.

Originally, this land was part of a claim made by Jean Baptiste le Moyne, Sieur de Bienville, the city's founder, for himself. His claim included all the land from Bienville Street past Carrollton to the Nine Mile Point, and from the river to what is now Claiborne Avenue. The grant was confirmed by the Superior Council of Louisiana in March 1719. But in November 1719, a royal order followed stating that governors could not receive land grants except for "vegetable gardens." Bienville took a portion of his original grant, settled German families in farms there, and called it his "vegetable garden." The area described above as Lafayette City has since been referred to as the "Garden District."

THE IRISH CHANNEL

So many Irish immigrants settled in an area between the Garden District and the river that the area came to be called the Irish Channel. This settlement took place mainly between 1846 and 1856. The area is bounded roughly by Magazine, the river, Jackson Avenue, and Toledano. Actually, the Irish Channel was originally only one street, Adele Street, which ran only two blocks, from St. Thomas to Tchoupitoulas.

JEFFERSON CITY

Following the same pattern, the next adjacent lands going upriver, between Toledano and Joseph streets and the river and St. Charles Avenue, became incorporated in 1850 as Jefferson City, which was annexed to New Orleans in 1870. The plantations of Plaisance, Delachaise, St. Joseph, East and West Bouligny, Avart, and Rickerville originally occupied this area. In Jefferson City, butchers operating slaughterhouses and dairymen pasturing cattle were the mainstays of local employment.

This land, too, was originally part of Bienville's land grant.

CARROLLTON CITY

Continuing upriver was Carrollton City, originally the site of the McCarty Plantation, then in Jefferson Parish. A group of real-estate investors acquired the land in 1831, and a surveyor subdivided it in 1833. It became a vacation "getaway" after the New Orleans and Carrollton Railroad was completed in 1835. The suburb offered a racetrack, beer gardens, and the Carrollton Hotel at the foot of Dante Street.

In the 1800s, it was a separate city of hardworking Irish, German, and Italian families. The center of town was the river bend. Carrollton became incorporated as a town in 1843, and the county seat of Jefferson Parish in 1852.

In the mid-nineteenth century, the town of Carrollton began to extend Carrollton Avenue through the Mid-City swampland to the New Basin Canal, finishing the roadway in 1862, and thus making settlement possible on three-quarters of the "rim of the saucer" of New Orleans. Carrollton City was bounded roughly by Lowerline, the river, Monticello Avenue, and Earhart Boulevard. It was annexed to New Orleans in 1874.

The site of the World's Fair and Cotton Centennial Exposition of 1884 was a rural tract "between the edge of Uptown and the recently annexed City of Carrollton." The land thus described in the city newspapers was earmarked for the fair by the city of New Orleans. It ran from the river to St. Charles Avenue and was easily accessible by boat and by the New Orleans and Carrollton Railroad (the St. Charles Streetcar today).

In the 1920s, and long before, the streetcars traveled "the belt," making a complete circle from any stop. The route went along Carrollton Avenue to St. Charles to Canal Street, then turned on South Rampart to Tulane Avenue, and continued on Tulane back to Carrollton again, all for six cents.

UPTOWN NEW ORLEANS

After the fair, the city turned the fairgrounds into Audubon Park on the river side of St. Charles Avenue, an area with many oaks and little lakes, ideal for a Sunday stroll. Across St. Charles Avenue, the land was secured for the city's two outstanding universities, Tulane and Loyola. Thus the fair had provided the city with a park, two universities, and choice sites for homes for the affluent. By

Audubon Place, across St. Charles Avenue from Audubon Park, an exclusive residential neighborhood along a private street. When Tulane University failed to exercise an option on this land, a real-estate company purchased and developed it around 1890. (Courtesy Earl K. Long Library, UNO)

Alma Pigeon, author's mother, at sixteen on an office picnic in Audubon Park, 1920. She worked as a stenographer at Pan-American Life Insurance Company.

1920, both universities were flourishing and many mansions had been built in this exclusive neighborhood.

Uptown New Orleans, now listed in the National Register of Historic Places, is an enormous area that lies *between* the former cities of Lafayette and Carrollton, and is bounded by Louisiana Avenue, Tchoupitoulas, Lowerline, and Claiborne. It is located on the sites of a series of eighteenth- and nineteenth-century plantations. It includes the former Jefferson City, the Audubon Park, and the University Area.

This semicircular development along the Mississippi's natural levee populated the city on three sides, following the river as it wound around New Orleans.

THE NORTH SIDE

On the fourth side, the north side, were the Gentilly-Metairie ridges and the Esplanade Ridge. Esplanade Ridge is the largest of the historic districts, roughly bounded by Orleans Avenue, St. Bernard Avenue, North Rampart, and the rear property lines of the properties facing Moss Street and Bayou St. John.

On its lower end, Esplanade Ridge is adjacent to Faubourg Treme. Esplanade Avenue runs the length of this district. Greek Revival and Italianate houses were built along this avenue from the 1830s to the end of the nineteenth century.

BAYOU METAIRIE AND BAYOU GENTILLY

Metairie Ridge and Gentilly Ridge, which were high and dry, had been settled early in the city's history, some properties as early as 1708, before New Orleans *was* a city. Metairie Ridge became Metairie Road and Gentilly Ridge became Gentilly Boulevard (or Chef Menteur) but for centuries, the two bayous were connected. Together, they were a distributary of the Mississippi River that had broken away and been abandoned by the river to drift lazily through the city and, in time, to disappear. While they lasted, however, natural levees built up alongside them, high rich land that encouraged settlement.

Even before Bienville came, Bayou Metairie had broken away from the river at Kenner Bend about twenty miles above the Vieux Carré, straying eastward toward the Gulf, roughly parallel to the river. When the river abandoned the stream, the part west of town came to be called Bayou Metairie; the part east of town, Bayou Sauvage or Bayou Gentilly.

The Metairie-Gentilly Bayou was not important for water transportation but it was very important for the well-drained land that had built up in levees alongside it. The land provided a high, flood-free route into the city from the west on Metairie Road, and from the east on Gentilly Boulevard (or Chef Menteur Highway). Along both ridges, communities of farmers settled.

ALLARD PLANTATION

One of the plantations in the Metairie Ridge area was the Allard Plantation (now City Park), whose ownership had passed through many hands before it came to those of Jean Louis Allard, Jr. Corn and sugarcane were raised there but it was primarily a dairy farm. Allard's house faced Bayou St. John near the point where the bayou intersects with City Park Avenue. Allard mortgaged the land to finance a crop and lost everything. The land was sold in a sheriff's sale in 1845.

John McDonogh, the new owner, supposedly allowed Allard to live on the land until his death, which occurred two years later. Allard is buried there, in an unmarked tomb beneath the one remaining Duelling Oak. McDonogh himself died in 1850, leaving the land to the schoolchildren of New Orleans and Baltimore. The city of Baltimore soon gave up its right to the land.

THE MATTER OF A PUBLIC PARK

McDonogh's death came at a time when New Orleanians favored public improvements. The *Daily Picayune* suggested that the Common Council introduce "the matter of a public park in the rear of the city." These sentiments found favor with Mayor A. D. Crossman. The Common Council voted to lay out a park on the tract of the Allard Plantation.

By 1891, a group of Mid-City businessmen, who had connections with "Ring" politics, had wrested administrative control of City Park from the city. By the turn of the century, railway companies sponsored band concerts in the park, and hauled passengers to hear them. Electric lights provided breathtaking nighttime effects. A racetrack drew crowds from 1905 to 1908.

By the end of 1920, the park had doubled in size. By the end of the decade, it had tripled. City Park was in great shape financially and geographically during the twenties.

DEVELOPMENT OF MID-CITY

My parents' house was located at the edge of the Esplanade Ridge, between Mid-City and City Park. This was a new area, sparsely populated, and country-like. Its development was part of a building boom that was taking place in New Orleans in the twenties. It was not until then that the Mid-City area began to be settled, and the population began in earnest to expand lakeward.

The unmarked tomb of Jean Louis Allard, Jr., beneath the one remaining Duelling Oak in City Park. Allard, who owned the plantation that is part of City Park, died in 1847.

Many streets of early New Orleans were still paved with Belgian block in the twenties. New Orleans had no stone of its own and used these blocks, which had come over as ballast in European ships. (Courtesy Earl K. Long Library, UNO)

This could not have happened at all without the machinery necessary to drain the swamps of Mid-City, machinery whose use was concentrated in that area between 1897 and the 1920s. Mid-City is now thought to be comprised of Mid-Uptown, Broadmoor, and Mid-Downtown.

THE WOOD PUMP AND THE CITY DRAINAGE SYSTEM

It took the invention of a heavy-duty screw pump by a gifted engineer named A. Baldwin Wood to raise huge volumes of debris-laden water vertically and move it fast. Wood later became the general superintendent of the Sewerage and Water Board.

Draining the swamps was a Herculean task. A system of drainage canals had to be built to carry the displaced water to Lake Borgne and Lake Pontchartrain. Then levees had to be built to secure the newly drained land. Pumping caused the swamps to fall farther below sea level, and flood control became a matter of life and death. The river levees had to be raised and a series of dikes built along the lake to keep out tidal surges.

In 1899, Orleans Parish passed legislation to install its first pumping system, but it was 1913 before the first Wood Screw Pumps were installed, and 1928 when the second set of pumping stations went up. Even when the middle city had been drained, nothing could be built there without driving pilings to considerable depths. The same levees that surround the "saucer" of New Orleans and protect it from flooding also keep water in, so drainage is our most important and unique problem. Without it, the city would flood and disease would spread.

The Wood Pump revolutionized the geography, the urbanization, and the future of New Orleans, opening it to settlement in the middle areas which had formerly been uninhabitable. After the elaborate system of drainage was installed,

The original A. Baldwin Wood Screw Pump, a twelve-foot pump, was put into operation in the city's new pumping system in 1913-15. Wood, the inventor, sold these drainage pumps all over the world. In 1927, he designed fourteen-foot pumps, which could drain the city of 1,000 cubic feet of water a second.

The main waterworks pumping station and drainage powerhouse No. 2. In 1920, seven great pumping stations were in operation, draining 7 billion gallons per day, sending normal flow into Lake Borgne and flow from heavy storms into Lake Pontchartrain.

LAKE PONTCHARTRAIN

New Orleans Lakefront Airport

Industrial Canal

Chef Menteur

Inner Harbor Navigation Canal

Pontchartrain Park

90

Gentilly Blvd.

University of New Orleans 1964

Southern University

Franklin Ave.

Pontchartrain Beach Amusement Park 1939–1983

Lake Oaks 1964

Leon C. Simon Dr.

(Robert E. Lee Blvd.)

Elysian Fields Ave.

University of New Orleans 1964

London Ave. Canal

Lake Terrace 1953

Bayou St. John

Wisner Blvd.

Lake Vista 1938

City Park

(Robert E. Lee Blvd.)

Orleans Ave. Canal

Lake Shore Drive

Marconi Blvd.

East Lake Shore 1955

Adams Ave.

Canal Blvd.

Harrison Ave.

West Lake Shore 1955

Florida Ave.

Yacht Harbor

West End Blvd.

Marina

Pontchartrain Blvd.

Jefferson Parish

Orleans Parish

West End Park

Public and quasipublic land

Pre-1927 lakeshore

The New Orleans lakefront in 1926 and after. The natural shoreline of Lake Pontchartrain was a smooth curve (see dashed line). All land north of the line is fill, nearly all since 1927. Bayou St. John, once the main entrance to French New Orleans, now is only decorative. Unshaded areas are private residential, sold by the Levee Board to help pay for reclamation. (Map by M. L. Widmer)

New Orleanians began to see houses and automobiles in greater numbers, steel bridges, and greater expansion lakeward.

ALGIERS POINT, A CITY WITHIN A CITY

One of the most charming neighborhoods in New Orleans was (and is) Algiers Point, which lies on the west bank of the river opposite the French Quarter. It is bounded by the river on two sides, Slidell Street, and Atlantic Avenue. Because it grew up isolated from the rest of the city, it had its own traditions and ways of life, little influenced by life in the big city.

Algiers Point is a series of winding streets, their direction influenced by the bend of the river, which gave the neighborhood its name. The community grew slowly from its beginnings as plantations in the early nineteenth century. Later it depended on shipbuilding and repairs for its economy, and still later on the Southern Pacific Railroad.

Development took place from the river and the ferry landing toward Opelousas Street and Atlantic Avenue. The earliest houses were built in the Greek Revival style, but most of them were burned in the great fire of 1895. In the early part of this century, bungalows and Classical Revival houses dominated the architectural scene. Few houses have been built in Algiers Point since World War II.

Shotgun houses and corner grocery stores give a visual low-scale character to this area that moves along at a leisurely pace, supporting its churches, schools, and small businesses pretty much as it did at the turn of the century. Algiers dates back to 1719, when it was part of the land claimed by Bienville. Much of the city's history is tied to its slave auctions, slaughterhouse, and powder house, for which the streets are named. Algiers was annexed to New Orleans at the turn of the century, and in 1904, Martin Behrman was the first Algerine to become mayor.

The ferry route between Algiers Point and the Canal Street landing was the only means of communication between the West Bank and the East Bank until the Huey P. Long Bridge was built in 1935.

GENERAL FACTS ABOUT NEW ORLEANS
IN THE TWENTIES

In 1920, the population of New Orleans was 387,219. It was the largest city in Louisiana, a city of distinctly French and Catholic heritage. Blacks numbered 39 percent of the population.

The leading industries of Louisiana were sugar refining and lumber products, but petroleum was third, and by the end of the decade, would be first. Louisiana's per capita income was $131. A native French, Spanish, and black Creole population dating from colonial times, joined by a substantial number of German, Irish, and Italian immigrants in the nineteenth century, formed the New Orleans community in 1920.

In 1912, the Pizatti Gate was constructed at the Alexander Street entrance to City Park. All through the twenties, it reflected the best traditions of ornamental ironwork with a gilded flair. From supports on each side of the entrance sprang a three-dimensional arch with a chain of rosettes and the name CITY PARK illuminated. (Courtesy City Park Collection)

CHAPTER TWO

City Park Heads
for the Lake

*I think that I shall never see
A poem lovely as a tree.*

THE NEIGHBORHOODS ON the "rim of the saucer" to the north of the city—Lakeview, City Park, and Gentilly—could not all be pulled together until City Park, the central rectangle of land, was extended to the lake. Only then could Lakeview find easy access to Gentilly, and this took decades to become a reality. But it all began in the twenties.

In the twenties, City Park tripled in size, becoming a solid rectangle of land between City Park Avenue and the lake, flanked by Lakeview on the west and Gentilly on the east. And this is how it happened.

To begin with, on June 11, 1920, the old City Park Race Track land (the site of today's Tad Gormley Stadium) became the property of City Park. By its acquisition and the purchase of several other tracts, the park took on an additional 180 acres, doubling its size and making it one of the largest urban parks in the nation.

North of the racetrack site was an enormous piece of land stretching from the racetrack property to the lake. It consisted of 900 acres, the largest segment of what is now City Park. At the southern end of this property were the tracks of the New Orleans Terminal Company, a Southern Railroad subsidiary.

New Orleans Land Company had held this property for speculation for years. For about a century before they acquired it, it had been used primarily for dairy farming. So much milk and cream cheese was produced in this area that the City Park Streetcar, which carried the cream cheese to the French Market, was called "The Cream Cheese Line."

Before 1920, City Park had no funds to buy the land, but feelers had been put out by the Park Board in case the money became available. In 1923, the Land Company agreed to hold the land off the market until the city could buy it.

In 1925 the Park Board asked the Land Company to fix a price of $2,000 per acre on the land, or a total of $2 million. Then when Martin Behrman made his fifth and final inaugural address in 1925, he promised a program of public improvements that included "the purchase of property that would extend City Park to the lake."

Behrman died in 1926. He did not live to see the passage of the bond election, but he made his mark on the history of the city by proposing the "City Park Extension." After the addition of this land, City Park reached from Bayou St. John to the Orleans Canal and from City Park Avenue to the lake. The lake began just beyond Robert E. Lee Boulevard in the early twenties.

In 1926, City Park covered 1,300 acres from City Park Avenue to the lake. Shortly thereafter, the Levee Board began to add land to the lakefront—with sand from the lake bottom—which would in time provide sites for five residential subdivisions, a boat marina, an amusement park, and an airport. The subdivision that would extend into the lake beyond City Park would be Lake Vista.

Although this land reclamation project began in the late twenties, the residential development of the new lakefront would not come until after World War II.

A Jahncke tugboat towing barges in the New Basin Canal was a familiar sight to Lakeview residents in the twenties. This scene is of the Old Shell Road tollgate near Metairie Cemetery (Old Shell Road is now Pontchartrain Boulevard). (Courtesy Lloyd W. Huber for the late Leonard V. Huber)

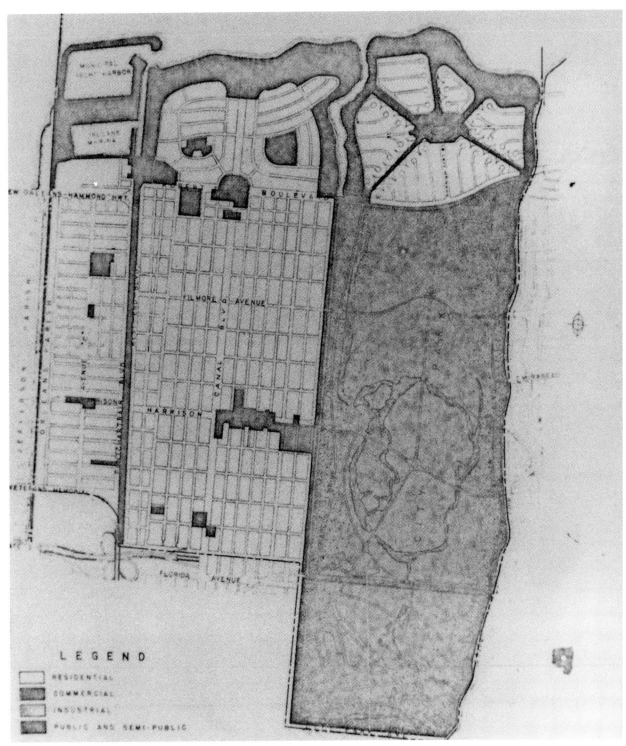

LEGEND

RESIDENTIAL

COMMERCIAL

INDUSTRIAL

PUBLIC AND SEMI-PUBLIC

This map of Lakeview was made in 1970 after a survey by the New Orleans Planning Commission. In the 1920s, Lakeview (left half of map) extended only to Robert E. Lee Boulevard (then Adams Avenue). Beyond that was the lake and many camps on piers. In the late 1920s, the reclamation program began, which would, in time, provide a yacht harbor and boat marina, and three new residential subdivisions beyond Lakeview and City Park (shaded right half of map). (Courtesy Lloyd W. Huber for the late Leonard V. Huber)

GIVEN·TO·THE·LITTLE·CHILDREN
OF·NEW·ORLEANS
BY
SARA·LAVINIA·HYAMS
MCMXIV

The statue at the Hyams Fountain and Wading Pool completed in 1921 depicts a happy family appropriate to the setting. It still stands in the center of the picnic grounds at City Park. (Courtesy City Park Collection)

CITY PARK IN CLOVER IN THE TWENTIES

All through the twenties, City Park prospered. Endowments poured in for sculptures and beautification projects, concerts and moving pictures. City Park also had the only public golf course in town.

In addition to the many bequests of money made to the park, there were special gifts bestowed during the decade. A new bridge that crossed a lagoon behind the Delgado Art Museum (today, the New Orleans Museum of Art) was given by Felix Dreyfous in 1923. A $60,000 swimming pool was donated anonymously by William Ratcliff Irby in 1924. And in 1928, a $25,000 gift from Rebecca Grant Popp and her sister, Isabel Grant, paid for a memorial fountain, several large shelters, and outdoor lighting.

Benevolent organizations such as the Elks, Kiwanis, and the Knights of Columbus sponsored the annual orphans picnics and the summer concerts on the bandstand near the peristyle.

With financial prosperity came the opportunity to upgrade the grounds, provide maintenance, and install new facilities, including two football fields, four basketball courts, and fifteen tennis courts. The children's playground area was expanded, and in 1923, a refreshment building was constructed nearby which came to be known as the "Little Casino."

BOATHOUSES ON BAYOU ST. JOHN

Numerous boathouses, squatters' cabins, house boats, shipyards, and boatworks clung to the shores of Bayou St. John in the thirty-year period between 1908 and 1938.

Four rows of Canary Island palms graced Anseman Avenue in City Park in 1925. The bare-breasted statues in front of the rows, which came from the Cotton Exchange, caused much outrage, and were soon removed to the Metairie Cemetery. (Courtesy City Park Collection)

A bronze reproduction of the nineteenth-century statue of Hebe, the Olympian cup bearer, by the Danish sculptor Thorwald, gazed down Lelong Avenue for fifty years after 1928, when Commodore Ernest Lee Jahncke donated it to the park. (Courtesy City Park Collection)

House boats, boathouses, and other craft crowded Bayou St. John in the twenties when litigation was in progress for control of the waterway. (Courtesy Lloyd W. Huber for the late Leonard V. Huber)

Until 1908, the Carondelet Canal Company had maintained the bayou, collecting tolls for its use, but then its charter expired. The state demanded control of the canal, its turning basin at Basin Street, and Bayou St. John, into which it flowed. Liquidators for the Canal Company refused the state's demands, and thus began a twenty-two-year legal struggle for control of the bayou.

Although it was under the jurisdiction of Congress to control commerce on this "navigable waterway," the Army Engineers did nothing so long as litigation continued. Since no authority was being exercised over the bayou, the area along Moss Street near Esplanade became a busy, noisy neighborhood of boathouses and cabins moored to the shores or anchored just offshore, where families hung out their wash, came aboard with groceries, and exchanged greetings with fishermen on the Esplanade Bridge or the Black Bridge (the railroad bridge toward the lake).

The Carondelet Canal was filled in between 1927 and 1938. Most of Bayou St. John came under the jurisdiction of the City Park Board in 1934. House boats were then ordered out of the area, and plans were made for the channelization and beautification of this historic bayou.

Members of the Irwin family enjoyed their porch at 2337 Valmont Street in the evenings in the twenties. From L: Edward M. Irwin; his wife, Viola; his sister Margaret Irwin; his daughter, May Irwin; and his sister Anna Irwin. (Photo by Charles L. Franck; courtesy John S. Burke, Jr.)

CHAPTER THREE

Family Life:
"Outdoor" Plumbing and
Old Wood Stoves

Just Molly and me, and baby makes three.
We're happy in my blue heaven.

MY FATHER GREW UP in the 1200 block of Dauphine Street in the Vieux Carré, not leaving that neighborhood until he married in 1924. He told me much about family life in the teens and the twenties. My mother, at age eighty-nine, added her own childhood and teenage memories to his. The two sets of memoirs formed the basis of my mental picture of family life in those times, with dates and statistics supported by research.

By 1920, the Vieux Carré was an area of dirt and squalor. It was hard to imagine that the homes on these narrow streets had once been charming residences. They were in the last stages of decay. Few people imagined that such a large area could be renovated and few cared enough for the historic significance of the Old City to make the effort. Restoration vs. demolition and rebuilding would be an ongoing conflict for years to come.

Families of means moved to newer parts of town. Jackson Square had become seedy, and the Pontalba Apartments were derelicts with vagrants for tenants. The whole area was fast becoming a slum.

MY FATHER'S HOUSE ON DAUPHINE STREET

The house my father grew up in was much like all other French Quarter properties, set on land that measured thirty feet wide by sixty feet deep. The house was built from border to border, having party walls with the two neighboring houses. It was a two-story house, with a central corridor leading off into two rooms on each side.

Behind the house was a yard about fifteen feet deep, and on the back property line was another two-story building, called a dependency, with two rooms downstairs and two upstairs. In this building, the outhouse, laundry room, and cooking area were situated, keeping the heat and unpleasant odors away from the area where the family lived and slept. That was the way of life in the Vieux Carré.

"OUTDOOR" PLUMBING

When my father left home to get married in 1924, there was still no indoor plumbing in the Dauphine Street house. The outhouse in the dependency had a

Mike Yuspeh, three, on tricycle he got for his birthday, 1923. (Courtesy Mike Yuspeh)

37

A bridal shower in the mid-twenties given in the home of the late Michael and Mary Irwin. After Michael's death, his five unmarried daughters continued to live there. Mamie died before this event. Jo was absent. Nellie is third from left. Sixth from left is Violet Irwin Burke, niece of the five sisters and mother of the contributor. Eighth, the honoree, is unidentified. Highest in rear is May, sister of Violet. The lady with the glasses is Anna. Closest to the camera is Margaret. (Photo by Charles L. Franck, courtesy John Burke, Jr.)

Author's grandfather, Franz Sales Schultis, German-born watchmaker, in his office in the Ma-
checa Building (later Godchaux's), 1921. Watches hanging behind him are awaiting pickup.
Banjo clock on far wall still hangs in home of author's mother.

Capt. Louis Laguens, Sr. (left), was in charge of the firehouse on the corner of Washington and Magazine (late twenties). (Courtesy Lynette Vinet)

toilet that consisted of a hole cut in a wooden seat that rested above a container with a cement floor. These outhouse containers were emptied from time to time and the refuse carried away in barrels. The wagons that took the barrels away were called "Honey Wagons." My father often remarked that there was nothing "good" about the "good old days."

The Sewerage and Water Board had been created in 1899 to pump out the swamplands in Mid-City. Soon after the turn of the century, the first purification plant went up. The Board began building a sewerage system, installing bathrooms in new homes, and replacing the toilets in outhouses with flush toilets that emptied into cesspools. In these outhouses they also installed bathtubs with running water.

Creoles in the French Quarter objected violently to these installations, since they would be forced to buy water to flush the toilets. To save the measure, the law was amended to provide free water for flushing toilets in New Orleans. This amounted to about one-fourth of the water bill. Free water for flushing was not discontinued until 1967.

In the twenties, a photographer went from house to house with his goat and cart to take pictures of children. Here in 1923 are Mildred Laguens and Jeannette Ernst. (Courtesy Lynette Vinet)

Frank and James Datri, with sacks on their shoulders, worked as young men (fifteen and twenty-one) in the macaroni factory on the corner of Chartres and Barracks (1921). (Courtesy Ann M. Novakov)

A BATHROOM *INSIDE* THE HOUSE?

My mother recalls that in the house where she grew up on Ursulines Avenue, sometime in the teens, a toilet and bathtub were installed "inside the house." This astonished the old people, who could not imagine such an inappropriate accommodation in a place where people lived.

In my mother's house, a toilet and bathtub were installed in the bedroom occupied by her three male cousins. Having no precedent to go by, her aunt and uncle, like many other New Orleanians, installed these facilities in the bedroom itself, with no walls around them for privacy. When my father built his house on Orleans Street in 1927, he had a bathroom installed—a whole room with a door and a key and everything. A wonderful element of privacy and comfort was introduced in that marvelous era.

Everyone used chamber pots well into the thirties, since houses were hard to heat, and people were reluctant to leave the warmth of their rooms during the night. *Pots de chambre,* or chamber pots, were kept under or alongside the beds, and used by children when needed during the night.

FRESH WATER CAME FROM CISTERNS

My father said that prior to the installation of household plumbing facilities by the Sewerage and Water Board early in the century, the only running water was river water. It was piped throughout the city, unpurified, and was very dirty. For fresh water, his family had a cistern in the yard.

The cistern was an oversized barrel about eight feet in diameter and ten feet high, made of wooden staves and equipped with a spigot about three feet above the ground. All the gutters from the roof drained into the cistern, and the dirt along with it, but there was a filter that removed most of the impurities, and no one worried too much about it.

According to my mother, who was born in 1904, only one or two people in the block on Ursulines near Claiborne had a cistern. She can recall nothing but piped water being used in her family's home for all purposes. And it was clean. Perhaps the age of the neighborhoods (the Vieux Carré was older than Faubourg Treme) might account for the difference in facilities.

My friend Ruby Boudreaux, born in Houma, Louisiana, in 1919, says that in the country, everyone used cistern water for drinking, bathing, and cooking. She recalls that as children growing up in the twenties, she and her sister would clean out the cistern once a year, since they were the only ones small enough and capable enough to accomplish this task. First her father would drain the cistern. Then he would put one ladder on the outside of the cistern and one on the inside. The girls would climb up and then down into the cistern, and with the aid of scrub brushes, remove the residue on the sides and bottom of the cistern. It was then rinsed well. Afterward, fresh and clean, it was allowed to fill with rainwater for general use.

Ruby also says that in the country, she and her siblings gathered moss, which was then washed and dried on clotheslines, then stuffed into mattresses. My mother says she can never remember sleeping on anything but cotton batting mattresses. But then, Mother was a city girl.

At the turn of the century, there was no drainage in the streets, but there were open wooden gutters all around each city block bordered by sidewalks. Early in the nineteenth century, wooden sidewalks had been replaced by brick. Street cleaners, called "White Wings," cleaned out the gutters periodically, but in the meantime, they were always full or half-full of stagnant water, garbage, and filth. In 1908 and 1909, the Sewerage and Water Board had begun to build its system of pumping stations and drainage canals to take care of the problem. After 1913, drainage gutters disappeared and streets ran from curb to curb with sewers set into the curbs at intervals to drain off into underground pipes and prevent flooding after heavy rains.

The heaviest rains were in 1925, 1926, and 1927, culminating in the record-breaking Good Friday rainstorm of 1927, when fourteen inches fell in twenty-four hours. The drainage system was inadequate to cope with the resulting flooding in many sections, especially Broadmoor, where it was flooded for two or three days. A second set of drainage canals was constructed in 1928 to prevent a reoccurrence of such flooding.

After a record fourteen inches of rain fell in twenty-four hours on Good Friday of 1927, almost all New Orleans was flooded. This is the corner of Iberville and Bernadotte. In 1928 came new pumps for better drainage. (Courtesy Maude Puissegur)

The sidewalks were called *banquettes* well into the thirties. The word is from the French, meaning a small bench. This makes sense, since each city block was an island surrounded by gutters; the sidewalk, together with the gutter, resembled a small bench. Some streets were made of Belgian blocks that had been used as ballast in ships coming from Europe. The city offered a premium for rock ballast, since there was no stone near the city. It was laid in a pretty diagonal pattern that eventually disappeared.

Streets were also made of gunwale, from flatboats that had come downriver before the era of steamboats. They had to be sold along with the merchandise, since they could not go back upriver against the current. Some streets were cobblestoned.

The first paving with square granite blocks was done in 1850 but on only one or two streets. By the 1920s, several hundred miles of streets were paved but an equal number remained unpaved. The kinds of pavement used were asphalt, mineral rubber, wood block, and granite rock. For an asphalt-topped street, a base of concrete was first laid, then a layer of tar and crushed stone, then a final layer of river sand and asphalt. The best kind of pavement for heavy traffic was creosoted wood block, made of pine blocks of uniform size. Such a street could take heavy traffic; it was noiseless, sanitary, and endured enormous weights without injury. By 1929, there were almost three hundred miles of paved streets in New Orleans.

STREET LIGHTING AND HOME LIGHTING

By 1920, in some parts of the city, arc lights at street intersections were being replaced by incandescent lights along the block. My husband's grandfather, Henry Widmer, was one of the pioneers in electricity in New Orleans. He had his own electric business in the French Quarter, where he rewound motors and repaired electrical wires. As a child, my father went with his father to Widmer Electric Company, coincidence being the astonishing thing that it is. That little boy of eight or nine years old would someday grow up and have a daughter (that's me) who would marry the grandson of Old Man Widmer of the electric company. Amazing!

Electricity was not in general use for house lighting until the early 1900s. The house my father lived in as a boy in the early century was illuminated by gas. He recalled ceiling gas fixtures in the parlor and dining rooms, fixtures that were electrified around 1912. These were originally brass gasoliers, with a pipe coming down from the ceiling to about six feet from the floor, having four or five branches, each with a separate gas jet. His father used tapers inside cylindrical handles to light the fixtures. In other rooms, there were gas fixtures in wall sconces made to look like candles.

When my father was twelve (in 1912), the Consumers' Electric Company installed electric light fixtures in their home. What a miracle! The company advised its patrons that they were allowed to burn four light bulbs at one time for an unlimited length of time for $1.00 a month. If you lit the fifth, the fuse would blow. But how elegant it was to flick a switch and get light—without a match, and brighter light than they had ever had before! The first few days, my father said, they went around flicking light switches with delight and astonishment. These light bulbs hung bare for the first few years, until some entrepreneur conceived the practical and aesthetic advantages of lampshades and lighting fixtures similar to the old gasoliers.

The Burke Electric Company, 1929. Author's father-in-law, Henry Widmer, is second from right. These shops wound electric motors and repaired electrical wiring. Henry Widmer's father, also Henry Widmer, was an electrical pioneer in New Orleans, owner of the Widmer Electric Company, and associate of Thomas Edison.

When the light bill was received on the first of each month, it was truly just a "light" bill, not covering any other electric appliances, since there were none.

This same company, organized in 1905, operated every street railway (streetcar) in New Orleans, as well as an electric light plant and a gas plant. It controlled twenty-nine streetcar lines. The fare was six cents, and a system of transfers allowed passengers to reach great distances without additional cost. The company furnished electrical current for lighting and power; its gas mains ran everywhere, as gas was used for fuel and heating as well as lighting.

TELEPHONES AND APPLIANCES

"In 1905, our first telephone was installed," my father wrote in his memoirs. "We were advised by the Cumberland Telephone Company not to let anyone but members of our immediate family use the phone. We got the feeling that the operator would be listening in, and if we disobeyed their orders, they'd come back and yank out our precious telephone. Of course, they were just trying to get new subscribers. In time, realizing this, we let our neighbors use the phone and took messages for those who had no phones."

It is easier to say what appliances people *didn't* have in the twenties than what they did have. Radios came into commercial use in the early twenties, but they started off with the crystal sets, and there was certainly not a radio in every home in 1920.

There were no electric fans in my father's home in the first two decades of the century, but the electric fan had been invented. In some few homes in the twenties, there were washing machines with wringer attachments on top consisting of two cylindrical rubber rolls that squeezed the water out of the laundry as it passed between them. But there were no clothes dryers or dishwashers, electric refrigerators or freezers. What *were* available in great abundance were Negro washwomen plying their trade at the French Market. They did "day's work" from sunup to sunset for fifty to seventy-five cents a day and their dinner.

MONDAY WAS WASHDAY

Clothes were usually washed on Monday in large washtubs, using washboards, Octagon bar soap, starch, bluing, and lots of elbow grease. One washtub was used to boil water over a charcoal furnace. In this tub, the scrubbed sheets and towels were boiled, then removed with a clothespole to a tub of clear water to rinse.

Clothespoles were straight, sturdy tree branches or barks split by a natural V at the top. They were used to lift the wire clothesline when it was weighted down with wet sheets pegged onto it with wooden clothespins. A clothespole vendor came around regularly selling these poles.

GROCERIES AND LAGNIAPPE

My father recalled *lagniappe* in his memoirs, but that was still in effect in my own childhood in the thirties. Lagniappe was a gift, something the butcher or grocer might give a customer without charge, to thank him for his patronage. A butcher might give you a sprig of parsley for lagniappe. A grocer might let the customer's child have a lollipop.

The clothespole man's cry was "clo-o-othespoles." Before the clothes dryer, laundry was hung out to dry on slack clotheslines, which were then raised and made taut by clothespoles. The poles were saplings, cut and trimmed of branches except near the top, where several were left to serve as Vs to hold up the line. (Courtesy Lloyd W. Huber for the late Leonard V. Huber)

Even on vacation at Little Woods, there was laundry to hang. These piers extended out over the lake, with porches surrounding the living areas. (Courtesy Lynette Vinet)

Frank Mustacchia and Sons' Grocery Store on Washington and St. Thomas. Refrigerators hold hams and liver loaf. Standing cases hold wine bottles. L to R: Joe Mustacchia, Nicholas Chisesi, a man named Jesto, John Mustacchia, policeman, and helper Sammy holding feather duster. (Courtesy the late Vita Chisesi Puissegur)

On every second or third corner in the French Quarter, there was a grocery store. Daddy ran errands to Matassa's for his mother, and was given a piece of hard candy from a small barrel. He remembered loaves of French bread piled high on the counter unwrapped. He recalled a wheel of cheese uncovered on the counter, or covered with a glass dome. Pickles were in open barrels, and so were beans. One grocery had a barrel of syrup, from which you filled your own pitcher. The barrel had a spigot on the side, which was always surrounded by flies, as was the sawdust on the floor beneath it. None of this had changed by 1920.

CHIMNEY SWEEPS

In the older houses of the Vieux Carré, as late as the twenties every room had a fireplace with a chimney. Even the cheapest double houses had them. Charcoal, burned in the grate fire, was purchased by the bucket from the corner grocery.

At least once a year, chimney sweeps were employed to clean the soot out of the flues. This specialist used a bunch of stripped palmetto fronds attached to a weighted rope to do his work. His trademark as he walked through the neighborhoods was his battered top hat. And his cry was in French: "R-r-ramoner la cheminée!" ("Sweep the chimney!")

Every fireplace had a mantelshelf, which was decorated with a lambrequin, a crocheted scarf edged with fringe that hung down ten or twelve inches from the shelf. It seems remarkable that they didn't often catch fire from sparks. Perhaps they did.

On this scarf sat a mantel clock as a centerpiece. "Chimney pieces" also adorned the corners of the mantel. These were sets of "whatnot" shelves about three feet high, connected by spindles, which flanked the mantel clock, holding statues, vases, and other treasures to be admired and to gather dust. Behind all this was a mantel mirror.

OTHER METHODS OF HEATING THE HOME

Many houses used steam heat given off by radiators in each room. Many New Orleanians used kerosene to heat their homes. The kerosene heater was a cylindrical tank standing on three legs. The top half could be lifted off, revealing a container for the kerosene in the bottom and a ring of jets that were lit with a match. Then the top would be placed back on. It gave off good warmth and was reasonably safe, as safe as most other heaters of the time.

All this was before the introduction of natural gas. Of course, people who built expensive homes had natural gas available to them since the middle of the nineteenth century. It had been introduced by James Caldwell in his American Theater in the 1820s, and he had obtained a franchise for installing gas heating in homes soon thereafter. New Orleanians are slow to change, however, and it wasn't until 1927, when my father built his own home on the Orleans Canal, that he had natural gas piped into his home for cooking and heating.

WOOD STOVES FOR COOKING

My mother described wood stoves to me, and said they were the only kind her family used until she married in 1924 and moved into a new house with a gas stove. The wood stove was a four-burner stove of black metal with a door on the

The chimney sweep traditionally wore a battered top hat and announced his coming with a call: "R-r-ramoner la cheminée!" ("Sweep the chimney!") Houses were heated by coal burned in a grate fire, and the chimney sweep was needed to clean the flues of soot. He did this with palmetto fronds attached to a weighted rope. (Courtesy Lloyd W. Huber for the late Leonard V. Huber)

In 1920, before citywide use of natural gas, New Orleanians used kerosene to heat their homes. These drivers are ready to begin their routes, their wagons loaded with one-gallon "safety" containers of "Stanocola Burning Oil." (Photo by Charles L. Franck, courtesy Lloyd W. Huber for the late Leonard V. Huber)

right-hand side, into which the wood was placed. A woodbin was kept on the floor alongside, in which split wood pieces in suitable sizes were kept available. The wood was placed in the stove through the side door, and a match applied to it through the burners. Burners were iron plates on top of the stove that could be lifted up with a curved iron bar that fit into a slot in the burner.

Burners were lifted to light the fire and to check its condition from time to time. The wood stove gave off a hot fire and cooked well, but I can imagine that while the kitchen must have been cozy in winter, it must have been a blazing inferno in summer. For that reason, many stoves were kept in the dependencies.

THE ICEMAN COMETH

As children playing outdoors in the hot New Orleans summers, both my mother and father waited for the iceman to come, so they could beg or steal a chunk of ice to chew on or apply to the head and face as a cooling agent.

With no electric refrigeration, the housewife had only the icebox, a wooden cabinet with three doors opening onto inner compartments (for ice, meat, milk,

This ice wagon was the property of the Solano Ice Company at 1529 Saratoga Street. Proprietor Joe Solano is holding the ice. He delivered wood, coal, and ice to customers in New Orleans in the twenties. The other men are not identified. (Courtesy Leslie Blanchard and Gail Tollin)

and produce). Some iceboxes were made with two large doors, one opening onto the top compartment for ice, the other onto the bottom for refrigerated items.

The iceman came every day, selling his patrons a twenty-five- or fifty-pound block, as needed. These he carried from his truck to the rear of the house by means of huge iron ice tongs. He then put the heavy block into the icebox for the housewife. His strength must have been prodigious, and his arms must have grown in length with his years as an iceman.

MAIL DELIVERY

In the twenties, mail was delivered to your door only if you lived along a well-defined street, had a *banquette* for the mailman to walk on, and a mailbox. Otherwise, you had to have a post office box, and you had to pick up your own mail. The city was growing so fast and in so many directions that the post office had a hard time keeping up with new neighborhoods and new street names.

Mail deliveries to those who qualified, however, were made twice a day (five times daily in the business district). The post office had three substations by 1920: Station A in Algiers, Station B on Napoleon and Prytania, and Station D at 3214 Dauphine Street. The post office occupied the lower floor in the Custom House from 1860 to 1915, when it moved into the beautiful new building on Camp Street, opposite Lafayette Square.

THE CATHOLIC CHURCH, A SIGNIFICANT FORCE IN NEW ORLEANS

Archbishop John W. Shaw became head of the Catholic Church in New Orleans in 1918. Under his guidance, the number of parishes grew to fifty-two in the city by 1929, each having a church and a school. The city had a total of 275 priests.

Seniors at Sophie B. Wright High School perform a minuet at the New Orleans Public School Historical Pageant, April 1920. (Courtesy Nora O. Ibert)

May Festival at Beauregard School on Canal Street and St. Patrick, 1929. (Courtesy Maude Puissegur, fifth girl from left)

St. Aloysius High School for boys, corner Esplanade and Rampart, lit up for a night activity. Operated by the Brothers of the Sacred Heart, the school celebrated its 100th anniversary in 1969 when it closed its doors. The building was torn down in the summer of 1969. (Courtesy Brother Martin High)

By decade's end, there were eight Catholic colleges and high schools for boys, and thirteen Catholic academies and high schools for girls. In 1922, the seminary for Catholic priests on South Carrollton Avenue was dedicated. It is one of the city's most beautiful buildings. By 1930, it had an enrollment of fifty students.

Mayor Arthur J. O'Keefe presents key to the city to movie producer Louis B. Mayer of Culver City, California, 1927. (Courtesy Nora O. Ibert)

CHAPTER FOUR

Ring Politics: "Papa Behrman's Back!"

Gambling and prostitution flourished [in the twenties and the thirties].
Police were on the take. Most government jobs were held by patronage.
Sports, show business, and misfortune (if not tragedy) occupied the atten-
tion of the readers of the city's newspapers.
                    F. Edward Hebert, from *The Last of the Titans*

MARTIN BEHRMAN, MAYOR OF NEW ORLEANS for the first one-fifth of the century, captured the imagination of the voters. My father knew no other mayor from his
birth in 1900 till his twentieth birthday, and Behrman was not through yet.

Behrman was orphaned at an early age and ended his formal education at St.
Philip School. He lived in Algiers, where he worked in a family grocery store
until he was married at the age of twenty-two. At that time, he became clerk in
the district assessor's office, a job that would be a political stepping stone to the
mayor's office. He had been backed by the Regular Democratic Organization
(RDO), but when Joseph A. Shakspeare became mayor in 1888, his "reform"
administration replaced all the RDO men with "reform" followers. Then when
John Fitzpatrick (RDO) defeated Shakspeare, the tables were turned again. This
time, Behrman was appointed clerk to three city council committees and elected
delegate to the constitutional convention in 1898, and state auditor in 1904.
Later in 1904 he was elected mayor of New Orleans by a landslide.

Behrman was reelected in 1908, 1912, and 1916. The RDO (also called the
Choctaw Club) was a smaller version of New York's Tammany Hall, a political
machine that seemed invincible. "Ring" politics grew stronger as Behrman won
election after election.

Most honest citizens considered "ring" or "machine" politics an iron fist that
kept everyone voting the prescribed way for fear of losing his job. My father, for
one, often railed against the Old Regulars, characterizing them as a bunch of
crooks. He was always on the side of the "reform" ticket, but he felt manipulated
and he never told anyone who he was going to vote for.

In 1920, John M. Parker, a reform candidate, was elected governor, and he
launched a movement to oust Mayor Behrman, who had been asked by the Old
Regulars to run for mayor for a fifth term. Behrman lost the election to Andrew
McShane in 1920, but was reelected in 1924. His supporters changed their campaign rallying cry from "Papa's Coming Home" to "Papa's Back." Behrman died
in office in January 1926, having served as mayor for seventeen years, the only
mayor in the city's history to have been elected five times.

Mayor Arthur J. O'Keefe, a city commissioner at the time of Mayor Martin Behrman's death in 1926, took over the reins of city government. The same year, he was elected to a four-year term, but he left office in 1929 because of illness. (Courtesy the late Eleonora O'Keefe)

No matter what history might say of Behrman, he was a man who rose from obscurity to power and enjoyed great personal popularity. Promised improvements became reality during his administration. He made available to the people a pure water supply, much needed sewerage and drainage systems, an enlarged public school system, improved fire and police departments, and the Public Belt Railroad and Parkway Commission.

Mayor Arthur J. O'Keefe, Sr., a city commissioner at the time of Behrman's death, was selected to fill Behrman's unexpired term in 1926. From the porch of his home on St. Mary Street, he recorded his voice for the inaugural Movietone News program at the Saenger Theatre. The same year, O'Keefe was elected to serve a four-year term, but he left office in 1929 because of illness.

O'Keefe had been born in the Irish Channel and had attended St. Aloysius High School. His work résumé is interesting and varied. He was a telegraph operator; later, he was active in the coffee and tea business; he served as vice-president of the American Bank and Trust Company; he held the office of city treasurer from 1912 to 1920; and he was in the State Senate.

O'Keefe was never in favor of Prohibition, an important issue during his administration. "If we ever leave it to the vote of the people," he said, "we'll be wet again. I remember those good old days when we could get big beers and we're going to get those good old days back."

Granted an indefinite leave of absence in 1929, he was replaced as mayor by T. Semmes Walmsley, who had been serving as commissioner of finance. Walmsley was elected in 1930 and reelected in 1934. His administration would take him

O'Keefe Coffee and Tea, on Magazine and St. Mary streets, was one of O'Keefe's enterprises before he became mayor of New Orleans. The owner's son, A. J. O'Keefe, Jr., ran the wagons and organized deliveries while attending Loyola Law School at night. (Courtesy Nora O. Ibert and Sheila Larson)

O'Keefe is at left in white suit, 1920. In this department, coffee is being weighed and bagged at 1904 Magazine Street. (Courtesy Nora O. Ibert)

This was the roasting room of O'Keefe Coffee and Tea, 1920. Workers are Albert Batiste and Charlie. (Courtesy Nora O. Ibert)

This was the "Premium Room," where coffee coupons were redeemed for prizes. (Courtesy Nora O. Ibert)

Mayor O'Keefe participates in the cornerstone laying of the new Raymond Telephone Exchange Building at 518 Baronne Street on April 5, 1927. L to R: Louisiana manager C. A. Stair, Mayor O'Keefe, an unidentified lady, F. R. Cordes, and W. J. Jenevein. Mayor O'Keefe was the father of Judge Arthur J. O'Keefe and the grandfather of Sen. Michael O'Keefe of New Orleans. Cordes was the father of Covington manager Paul Cordes. Jenevein was the uncle of Earl Jenevein, Covington engineer; the brother of Edwin P. Jenevein, retired state plant maintenance supervisor; and brother of the late George A. Jenevein, head cable splicer. (Courtesy Nora O. Ibert)

through the bank failure of 1929 and into the big depression. He was backed by
the Old Regulars, and was a political enemy of Governor Huey P. Long, elected
in 1928. After Long's death, Long's followers put pressure on Walmsley to resign
in August 1936.

For mayor of New Orleans, Long supported John Klorer, chief engineer for the
Orleans Levee Board, and in his openly insulting way, Long always referred to the
mayor as "Turkey Head" Walmsley.

HUEY P. LONG: A HERO WAS NEEDED

Late 1929 and the early thirties brought New Orleans unemployment, soup
lines, and worthless bank accounts. Like all other cities in the United States,
New Orleans was on the threshold of the Great Depression. People were beginning to lose hope, and a hero was needed. When Huey Pierce Long was elected
governor of Louisiana in 1928, and United States senator in 1932, Louisianians
felt that they had found that hero.

Long had built up one of the most powerful machines in the United States, and
in the face of incredible obstacles, put over his radical program by the sheer ex-
uberance of his personality. His doctrine was socialistic, a revolution of the poor
whites. "Every Man a King" and "A Chicken in Every Pot" were the slogans of his
"Share the Wealth" program. He preached with arms flung wide and fists coming
down on the podium with resounding blows.

EVERY MAN A KING

His message was that no man should be allowed to earn more than a million
dollars a year. Everything over that should go into a fund from which the needy
would be taken care of. Many hated him, but his power was such that his en-
dorsement for any political office in the state was tantamount to election. His
control of the legislature enabled him to pass his entire legislative program.

Every Man a King, a ghostwritten book, laid out the plans for his program. He
claimed to have written the catchy song of the same name, which was actually
written by Castro Carazo, the orchestra leader at the Strand in the twenties.

To the poor he was a saint. Louisianians were used to dictatorship of one kind
or another in the governor's office. If Long wanted to be their dictator, it was all
right with them. Hadn't he promised them free school books for their children?
Paved roads? A Mississippi River bridge? He rode into office on their votes.

He called himself "The Kingfish." He published his own newspaper, the *American Progress.* He wrote a second book, *My First Days in the White House,* a futur-
istic exercise in political egomania. He became a cult figure.

Long made many enemies in Washington, D.C. with his bombastic speeches
and his Mafia-like tactics. Senators would rise and leave the chambers whenever
he stood up to speak.

Huey P. Long was assassinated in the state capitol in Baton Rouge on September 8, 1935, allegedly by Dr. Carl A. Weiss, whose father-in-law had been gerry-
mandered out of office. Weiss was then riddled with bullets by Long's bodyguards.
Thousands wept at his lying-in, as endless lines moved slowly past his coffin.

Good vacation spots were camps over Lake Pontchartrain at the end of West End Boulevard at Adams Avenue (1923). (Photo by Charles L. Franck, courtesy Earl K. Long Library, UNO)

CHAPTER FIVE

Lake Resorts, Parks, and Amusements

By the sea, by the sea, by the beautiful sea
You and I, you and I, oh how happy we'll be!

IN THE EARLY TWENTIES, West End Park, Old Spanish Fort, and the summer camps at Milneburg were the only lakeside resorts in town. They were connected to the developed areas of the city by railroad lines or waterways. The land in between consisted of marshy cypress groves and swampland. Houses had been built in Old Lakeview but there was no Canal Boulevard as we know it with sunken gardens (that would come in the thirties), no Marconi Drive, and no Wisner Boulevard to give access by car to the lakefront from City Park Avenue.

As we have said, there was only the Old Shell Road, which took the motorist to West End Park, and the Smoky Mary railroad train, which took the passenger to Milneburg.

Winding pebble road to West End Park and Southern Yacht Club. West End Park was a popular lake resort from 1880 into the 1920s.

LET'S TAKE A RIDE TO WEST END

My mother and father took many a ride out to West End Park on the Old Shell Road in the twenties and thirties. The road was three miles long from City Park Avenue to Adams Avenue. A few more blocks and a black bridge over the New Basin Canal took the motorist to the oval-shaped park on the lakefront close by the Southern Yacht Club.

From their house on the Orleans Canal, they got to the Shell Road by driving along City Park Avenue to Metairie Road at the Halfway House (now Orkin). The Shell Road afforded a view of palm trees and oleanders, and of cargo and pleasure boats on the New Basin Canal. In the twenties, people used to take rides just for the pleasure and novelty of riding in a car. There was no home entertainment as we know it—television, stereos, and videos. Most people didn't even have radios in 1920 and 1921.

The Smoky Mary was a different kind of diversion. From the depot on Elysian Fields at the river (later from the L&N Station), it chugged along on a six-mile course through undeveloped swampland that was densely overgrown and frequently flooded.

AMUSEMENT PARKS ON THE LAKEFRONT

West End Park (originally called New Lake End) had been taken over by the city in 1871 when it was nothing more than an embankment 800 feet offshore in Lake Pontchartrain at the end of the New Basin Canal. By 1880, when it was rechristened West End Park, the New Orleans City and Lake Railroad had a steam train running out to the site, where they had built a hotel, a restaurant, and structures to house amusements. It was the city's most popular lake resort for the next thirty years.

In 1896, the first moving pictures seen in the city were shown on a large canvas screen in front of the bandstand. In 1898, the railway was electrified, and the six-and-a-half-mile ride from the city on the "West End train," a motorcar pulling several open-sided trailers, took pleasure-seekers from Canal and Elks Place to West End Park.

ROMANCE AT WEST END PARK

To inject a personal note here, it was at West End Park in 1897 that my German grandfather, then forty, first set eyes on my beautiful, blonde grandmother, a French girl fifteen years his junior. Old Paw-paw was a watchmaker with wanderlust who had been around the world three times, once on a bicycle, or so the family legend goes. He quickly made friends with her brother, wrangled a proper introduction, and his wandering days were over. Within a year they were married and expecting their first child.

I sometimes picture them having dinner at Mannessier's on the huge platform overlooking the lake or riding out to the resort on the open-air train.

SPANISH FORT COMPETES

In 1909, West End's monopoly on lakeside amusement ended. A disagreement between the city and the railroad line resulted in the railroad company's acquisition and development of the old Spanish Fort property, which would become a competitor to West End Park.

The city retaliated by making great improvements at West End. A seawall 500 feet farther out in the lake was built and filled in with sand from the lake bottom to form the thirty-acre West End Park. These improvements were completed in 1921.

West End Park in the twenties offered swings, slides, and seesaws for children, amusements to ride on, a bandstand for concerts, seafood restaurants, and other concessions. But its main attraction was its magnificent fountain, which drew people from all over town. It was situated in the center of a horseshoe of grass ringed by a paved street.

The fountain shot up dozens of jets of water, in a myriad of colors and heights, like a ballet of lights dancing to the music of cascading water. For a moment the jets would all be green and very low in height; then, suddenly, a huge central spray of ruby jets would fountain up fifty feet or more, and the spectators would gasp in chorus. The fountain was operated by one man, W. A. Dietzel, an electrical engineer who pulled levers and pressed buttons that controlled the lights and the jets. The fountain and West End Park itself entertained three generations in our family. But by the time I had my own children (the 1950s), the fountain was no longer in operation.

This multicolored electrical fountain was in the center of West End Park in the twenties. Every night, electrical engineer W. A. Dietzel operated the jets in height and color from a pump house. (Courtesy The Historic New Orleans Collection, acc. no. 1979.325.6311)

Spanish Fort Amusement Park on Bayou St. John and Adams Avenue, early twenties.

Over the Rhine, a restaurant situated across Bayou St. John from Old Spanish Fort, early twenties.

Spanish Fort, as a resort, had grown up around the site of an old colonial fort originally built by the French in 1701 at Bayou St. John and Lake Pontchartrain. Rebuilt by the Spanish in 1779, it was called Spanish Fort. It became a resort in 1823 when the government sold the fort as "surplus" to Harvey Elkins, who built the Pontchartrain Hotel within its walls.

By 1878, a railroad had been constructed to connect the resort to the city, the property had changed hands, and Moses Schwartz had built a casino where excellent meals were served for $1.00 and a theater featured light opera and band concerts. It went into disuse, however, when the railroad discontinued service in 1903 and its buildings burned in 1906. After New Orleans Railway and Light Company acquired the property in 1909, it rebuilt and reopened Spanish Fort as an amusement center.

Spanish Fort, at the turn of the century, boasted a beer garden, a bandstand, a restaurant, and concessions. The restaurant, called "Over the Rhine," was reached by a footbridge that crossed Bayou St. John and was opened manually to allow small craft to go by. (The bridge divided in half and folded parallel to the shore.) I remember crossing that bridge in the thirties.

When my mother and father went there in the late 1920s, the park had been relocated from Robert E. Lee Boulevard and Bayou St. John up toward the lake along the bayou. It was situated on the newly reclaimed land from the lake bottom. The reclamation was part of a project commissioned in 1924 to upgrade the levee and make the lakefront more attractive. A concrete seawall was being constructed five and a half miles long and approximately three thousand feet out into the lake from the old shoreline. The area in between, pumped from the lake bottom, created 2,000 acres of new land that was as high as any in the city.

The site of Spanish Fort later became Lake Vista, the first section of the lake-front to be used for a residential subdivision. But Spanish Fort Amusement Park was its first tenant. Its name was changed in 1928 to Pontchartrain Beach Amusement Park, but no one paid any attention. It was still Spanish Fort to New Orleanians.

The miles of new land along the lakefront from West End to the Shushan Airport were earmarked for public beaches, boulevards, and parks, which would be a great catalyst to lakeward residential expansion. All this would be delayed, however, by a depression and a war. Unable to foresee the heartaches that lay ahead, New Orleanians were enthralled with the plans for a beautiful new lakefront.

Concessions at Spanish Fort in the late twenties made it more of an amusement park than a resort. Flying horses, a Ferris wheel, the Wild Cat, a penny arcade, and rides like the Bug were set up along a boardwalk edging Bayou St. John. A long pier stretched out into the water so that bathers could walk out to where the water was at least hip deep before climbing down the steps to swim. Bathhouses were available and families came for the day, bringing picnic lunches, which they arranged on tables under the roof of a large pavilion.

In the twenties, ownership of the Spanish Fort property reverted to the city, and the amusement park was under the control of the Levee Board. The Board decided to establish a permanent site for an amusement park a few miles east at the end of Elysian Fields Avenue. The Batt family gained control of the park in 1934, and in 1939 moved into the beautiful new Pontchartrain Beach Amusement Park, which flourished until 1983.

Bathing at Pontchartrain Beach, off the pier near the end of Bayou St. John, was great fun in the twenties. (The name was changed from Spanish Fort to Pontchartrain Beach Amusement Park in 1928.)

Bathing pier of Spanish Fort; a bathhouse is to the rear.

VACATIONS AT MILNEBURG

My mother was an only child, so in her youth (1910-20), she and her parents, along with her aunts and uncles and cousins, rented a camp every summer at Milneburg. There they swam and crabbed or just sat on the porch enjoying the lake breezes. This land was later Pontchartrain Beach Amusement Park, and still later, the University of New Orleans.

Vacationers could ride out to the camps at Milneburg on a railroad train mentioned earlier, pulled by an old engine affectionately called the "Smoky Mary." It was part of the Louisville and Nashville Railroad. When the Smoky Mary made its last run to the lake in 1932, I was a little girl sitting on my mother's lap. Mother took the last trip out of nostalgia for by-gone days.

The camps, built on stilts and approached by long slatted piers, ran side by side out over the lake like hundreds of centipedes at a starting gate. Many camps were connected to one another by additional piers, for easy communication for families and friends. Seen from the air, the whole colony of camps looked like a huge nest of spiders.

Each camp was built with bedrooms and a kitchen in the middle, and a huge wraparound screened porch for maximum enjoyment of the breezes off the lake. It was not unusual for cots to be lined up on the porches for sleeping, a total delight on a hot summer night.

The camps were owned and furnished mostly by sports fishermen, whose families used them for a day or two now and then, or a week or two in the summer. The rest of the time, they rented them out to city people eager for a change of scenery. Old-timers in New Orleans recall their vacations at Milneburg with great affection.

Alma Pigeon, author's mother, eighteen, poses with umbrella in 1922 at Milneburg Camp (where UNO is today).

Camps built out over Lake Pontchartrain just past Adams Avenue in the 1920s. (Photo by Charles L. Franck, courtesy Shushan Collection, Earl K. Long Library, UNO)

The Bianchini family at Little Woods (now New Orleans East) at a camp, July 4, 1927. (Courtesy Judy Pesses)

Camps extended out over the lake from West End to Paris Road in the twenties. The easternmost camps, beyond Shushan Airport, were in Little Woods, now part of New Orleans East. They are the only ones still in existence.

The 1928 plans for the development of the lakefront included the tearing down of all camps from West End to the Industrial Canal. Then came the building of the stepped seawall and the pumping of sand from the lake bottom into the extended lakefront. This would not be completed until the thirties with the help of WPA money and labor.

THE TOWNS "ACROSS THE LAKE"

From West End Park, passengers could take the pleasure boats *Susquehanna, Camellia,* and *Southdown* across the lake. Moonlight rides around the lake, with famous jazz bands for dancing, were also popular.

Another way to get across the lake was by car, by means of the Chef Menteur Highway. On the north shore of Lake Pontchartrain was St. Tammany Parish, with its pine forests and balmy breezes. The little town of Mandeville offered thatch-covered open-air booths with picnic tables all along the camp-lined North Shore, where families could relax for the day. Picnicking was popular in the twenties and thirties, what with the automobile new on the family scene, and neither television nor air-conditioning yet to drive families indoors.

A few miles farther by rail or auto brought you to the little town of Abita Springs, where people went to drink the waters of the pure crystal springs, to "take the baths," and to breathe in the fresh piney air.

The steamer Susquehanna *took passengers from New Orleans to Mandeville across Lake Pontchartrain, while jazz bands played.*

Nearby was the town of Covington, with its three romantic rivers: the Bogue Falaya, the Abita, and the Tchefuncte overhung with mossy oaks.

To get to Waveland, the easiest route was by way of the L&N Railroad, or by car. Many New Orleanians had houses in Waveland, where they spent time in the summer, swimming and crabbing. Five miles farther on was Bay St. Louis, with its huge white beaches, beautiful homes, schools, and colleges. Then across the Bay Bridge and into the woods, the little town of Pass Christian, called "The Pass," spread out its beautiful waterfront, and its row of two-story homes with wide galleries and magnificent oaks. Gulfport, the next town along the Mississippi Coast, boasted wonderful hotels, restaurants, and a continuing line of fine homes and trees with hammocks swinging lazily beneath them. Biloxi and Ocean Springs, the next towns along the coast, were two of the first towns founded by Iberville in 1699. Biloxi, with its hotels and boardinghouses, beaches and restaurants, its combination of the old and the new, was sought out by many New Orleans vacationers. Ocean Springs was more of a residential country town. The last major town on the Mississippi Gulf Coast was Pascagoula.

AMUSEMENTS IN CITY PARK AND AUDUBON PARK

The City Park swimming pool with its sun-drenched bathhouse and lines of lockers opened in 1925. The diving boards and central raft were inviting to New Orleans children. Parents supervised from park benches beneath shade trees outside the wire fences.

When children went on the amusements, the perennial favorites were the flying horses, housed in a beautiful building with stained-glass clerestory windows and a cupola, which has stood in the same spot since 1929; the miniature train,

LAKE RESORTS, PARKS, AND AMUSEMENTS

Audubon Park, also called "Upper City Park," was newly landscaped just before the twenties with grassy expanses, lakes, palms, and graveled footpaths.

Audubon Park in the twenties. An ancient oak reflects in a lagoon spanned by a wooden bridge.

Audubon Park, newly landscaped in the twenties, as seen from the top floor of Thomas Hall on the Loyola campus on St. Charles Avenue. (Courtesy Loyola University)

the park's second oldest ride, which operated in the twenties on a limited scale in the picnic area; the Whip, which came to the park in 1929; and the pony ring, which began in 1926.

Audubon Park, sometimes called "Upper City Park," was originally a plantation owned by Pierre Foucher and his wife, Françoise de Boré. Part of it had been purchased by Foucher from Charles Gayarré, the New Orleans historian, who had inherited it from his grandfather, Etienne de Boré, the first mayor of New Orleans. In the 1880s, a beautiful golf course was laid out and in the early 1900s, waterways and lagoons were added, as were grassy expanses interspersed with clusters of trees and footpaths to border three miles of winding bayous.

THE FIRST AUDUBON ZOO

The first zoo in Audubon Park was just a random collection of animals in cages along Magazine Street. In 1924, the zoo's first elephant arrived, a female, Itema, purchased for $3,500.

Also in 1924, the Park Commission opened fifty acres to baseball fields and other recreational facilities.

Perhaps the most popular facility was the Audubon Park swimming pool and bathhouse, which opened in the spring of 1928 at a cost of $250,000.

The sea lion pool was also built in 1928, as was the aquarium, which was an immediate favorite. The Teddy Roosevelt carousel, which delighted children in the twenties, had been built in Philadelphia in the famous Dentzel Carousel Factory and installed in the park in 1912.

By the end of the twenties, Audubon Park was not the urban oasis that designer Frederick Law Olmsted had envisioned. Times had changed. People wanted baseball fields, swimming pools, and tennis courts, not just beautiful landscapes.

In the twenties and thirties, when the greatest changes and the most progress were being made in both city parks, integration was still a thing of the future. Blacks were not allowed in the swimming pools, on the rides, on the tennis courts, on the golf course, or in the rest rooms. They *were* allowed in the zoo, but they had to keep moving. They could not sit on the benches. What a sad commentary on laws governing our black citizens at that time!

Interior of the Saenger, the "Florentine Palace," when it opened in 1927. Statues stand atop garden walls and marble fountains create the feeling of an outdoor garden at night. Stars twinkle in an azure ceiling. (Courtesy The Historic New Orleans Collection, acc. no. 1979.325.3920)

CHAPTER SIX

The Flickers and the
Moving Picture Palaces

He slept by day and roamed the world by night,
seeking victims in his endless quest for blood.
Local newspaper ad for *Dracula,*
the Undead (a silent movie)

MY MOTHER TELLS ME THAT in the early twenties, when she was working as a stenographer at the Pan-American Life Insurance Company, the most popular subject of discussion among the office workers was the movies. I'm sure that housewives also talked about them over coffee, and young mothers wheeling their babies in carriages discussed them in the park. Movies were the craze.

Mother can remember going to the Loew's Crescent on the corner of Baronne and Common streets when she and my father were dating in the early twenties. The building with the memorable arcade, which serviced both of the Twin Theaters—the Crescent and the Tulane—had been designed by Thomas Sully, who had also designed the third St. Charles Hotel.

The Tulane and Crescent Arcade was on Baronne and Common streets. Built in 1898, the Tulane showed legitimate theater; the Crescent showed vaudeville and movies. Torn down in 1937, the theaters were replaced by the Roosevelt annex, then the Shell Building, then the Exxon Building.

Tulane and Crescent Theatres, New Orleans, La.

The theater opened on Sundays at 12:30 P.M., and it advertised "Go Where the Cool Breezes Blow," always a drawing card in the hot Crescent City. Weekday matinees were ten cents; admissions on Saturdays and Sundays were ten cents, fifteen cents, and twenty-five cents, depending on where you sat and what time you arrived.

The Crescent offered movies and vaudeville: The Diminutive Star, La Petite Jenie, and The Dolly Dancers, to name but a few; a rendition by a symphony organ; Loew's News Events; Popular Comedies; a performance by the Loew's Orchestra; and a main movie feature, such as the one shown in June 1920, *My Little Sister: A Realistic Story of the City's Menace*, with Evelyn Nesbitt. It was quite a bill for twenty-five cents!

The Tulane was a legitimate theater, which featured such stars as the Barrymores and Katherine Cornell. Operettas came to the Tulane, such as *The Student Prince, The Desert Song, Blossom Time*, and *The Merry Widow*. Road shows making the rounds, like *Rio Rita* and *The George White Scandals*, played to packed houses, the latter due to the partial nudity of the actresses. Contrary to what we think today, nudity is not new to the stage, nor was it then.

As a child, I heard my mother talk frequently about the Tulane and Crescent theaters. The arcade could be entered from Baronne or Common streets. These two theaters were built in 1898 on the site where the original Tulane University had stood before it moved uptown. They were operated by Klaw and Erlanger, rivals of the Shuberts who owned the local Shubert Theater on Baronne Street, and of the Orpheum group that ran the St. Charles Theater at 432 St. Charles.

My husband's uncle, Phil Abadie, used to make us laugh with his stories about going to the matinee at the Tulane and "rushing the pit" (getting the best seat in the best section of "cheap seats"). He often quoted, in melodramatic vaudevillian style, the ending lines in a play he saw there. With her hand on her heart, the heroine emoted, "Whither thou goest, I will go; for your country is my country, and your God is my God!" They brought the house down with that one, Uncle Phil used to say.

By 1927, there were fifteen major theaters in New Orleans and fifteen nickelodeon movie houses. The town was mad about the flickers. On their "downtown" dates in the early twenties, my mother and dad usually took in a movie, then went to a drugstore like Fuerst & Kraemer's for a soda or a sundae. My father always loved vaudeville, especially the comedians. He loved slapstick comedy, and thus, he was easily wooed from vaudeville to silent films with stars like Charlie Chaplin, Buster Keaton, and Harold Lloyd to talking pictures with comedians like Laurel and Hardy, Patsy Kelly, Edgar Kennedy, and the Marx Brothers.

As movies took over and vaudeville waned, some of the theaters began going out of business. In 1937, the Twin Theaters were torn down, to be replaced by a parking lot, then the Roosevelt annex, then the Shell Building, and then the Exxon Building.

THE SAENGER AMUSEMENT COMPANY

In the early twenties, the Saenger Amusement Company owned the Strand Theater, on Baronne and Gravier; the Globe Theater, at 606 Canal Street; the Tudor, next door to the Globe; the Trianon, at 814 Canal, next door to the Boston Club; and the Alamo, at Canal and Rampart.

The Strand, which had opened in 1917, was a big first-run theater. It had an organ and a twenty-piece, full-time orchestra led by Castro Carazo. The Strand also boasted elegantly appointed rest rooms with private telephones, toilet accessories, and a maid in attendance. Not to be overlooked were its "swirling breezes, generated from giant typhoons" to keep its patrons cool.

The Strand had been built by entrepreneur E. V. Richards, president of the Saenger Amusement Company, who had come to New Orleans in 1917 and taken over the theaters of Fichtenberg Enterprises. When the Saenger Company gave up control of the St. Charles Theater, it made the Strand its flagship. Then, in 1927, when the company opened the Saenger Theatre on Canal Street, *that* movie palace became its flagship.

A local entrepreneur named Gaston J. Dureau published a newspaper for the Saenger Company offering gossip about movie stars and giving information on coming attractions. He soon became a film booker and an advertising and publicity manager for the company. He booked 140 movie theaters in the South and published *The Saenger Humdinger,* the company's official journal. A cartoon in a copy of the *Humdinger* in 1920 showed a recreation home, a plantation called Elmwood Manor in Bay St. Louis, which the Saenger Company offered to its employees to use during their vacations.

WHAT THE "SILENT MOVIES" WERE SHOWING

In 1920, the Trianon, on Canal Street, was showing Jess Willard, the former heavyweight champion of the world, in a picture that boasted "love, hard fighting, 3000 people, and hundreds of horses." It was called *Challenge of Chance,* and the admission was twenty-five cents, including war tax of three cents, a tax that had been levied during World War I and lingered in postwar days.

The Globe was showing *Happiness a la Mode* with Constance Talmadge, and a special musical program by the Tudor Orchestra. They cautioned women in their ads, "Hold onto your husbands. The first year of married life is the hardest. After that, you get used to it."

Beneath the double newspaper ad for the Trianon and the Tudor was a tempting addition: "Like a frothy summer confection, our ventilation keeps our theater COOL." My father said the movie houses were as hot as blazes.

HORROR IN BLACK AND WHITE

Horror themes were a natural for silent black and white movies. Even without the heroine's scream of fear, the flickers could show a monster, a beautiful woman who makes the monster aware of his vulnerability, and a hero who never quite manages to save the heroine. Over-made-up and overacting, these leading characters scared audiences to death. Close-ups were important. Producers wanted the viewers to see, in graphic detail, the horrors revealed to them.

The first version of *Dracula, the Undead* was seen in the silent flickers. "He slept by day and roamed the world by night, seeking victims in his endless quest for blood," the ads said. The movies may have been silent, but the people in the audience cried out.

In *Dr. Jekyll and Mr. Hyde,* made in the twenties, John Barrymore drank the potion and changed to a man as evil as the devil himself, but only his expression changed, not his physical appearance. He had to be a fine actor to carry it off.

Lon Chaney, the "Man of a Thousand Faces," often applied his own spectacular makeup. In the silent version of *The Phantom of the Opera,* much of the action took place in the catacombs beneath the city of Paris. Chaney's performance

77

was like ballet. He was a master of pantomime. When the beautiful diva unmasked his hideous face, he recoiled in shame because she had seen his disfigurement.

Long before the "talking" Frankenstein, a silent movie portrayed a mad scientist who wanted to create human life. Another "silent" showed a dark evil doctor who wanted to control life from afar, giving commands from a distance.

It is hard for us to realize that before 1927, the scream of the heroine had never been heard. It was up to the actors to make the audience shrink with fear, and up to the organist in the movie house to play the chilling music that characterized horror movies.

OTHER DOWNTOWN MOVIE SHOWS

The Lyric Theater, which catered exclusively to black New Orleanians, opened in February 1919, at the corner of Iberville and Burgundy streets. It was the largest theater of its kind in the United States (2,000 capacity). The weekly bill included movies, vaudeville, and newsreels. Its audiences enjoyed the talents of such notables as Mamie Smith, Florence Mills, and Josephine Baker.

The Palace Theatre for Negroes on Dauphine and Iberville as it looked in the twenties. Built in 1903 as the Greenwall Theater, it was a movie house called the Palace when demolished in 1963.

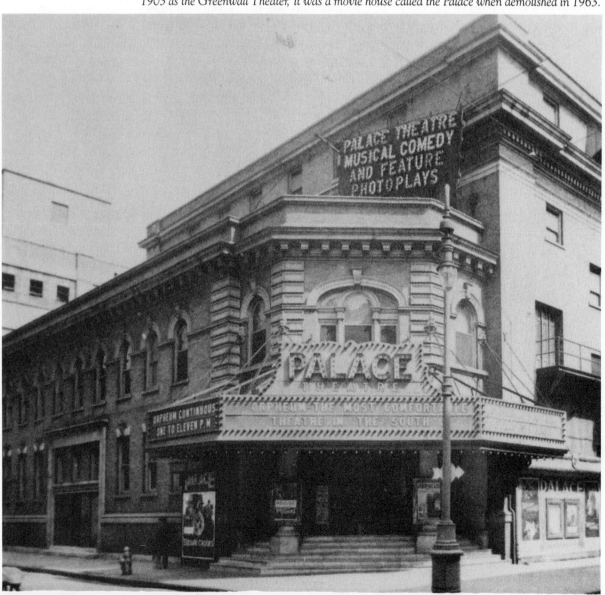

The Famous Theater on Marigny and North Claiborne, built in 1913, was rebuilt in 1927. The new building was constructed outside of and on top of the old, and the old Famous was not demolished until the new one was completed. (Courtesy Rene Brunet, Jr.)

In the early twenties, the theater at 533 Baronne Street, which boasted a beautiful arcade, was called the Star. It had previously been called the Shubert Theater when the Shubert Company operated it; then around 1910, it had become the Lafayette. The name *Lafayette* was painted on the front and can still be partly seen. In the twenties and thirties, it was the Star, then the Poche, and finally the Civic.

The theater was built by the Stone Brothers, Architects. Its arcade was later done by Toledano and Wogan. The nineteenth-century "champagne circle," the gold mirror in the foyer, the elaborate dressing rooms, and the enormous chandelier all helped make this one of the downtown movie palaces.

The Liberty was on St. Charles Street.

The St. Charles Theater, at 432 St. Charles, was the third St. Charles built on that site, the first two having been razed by fire. According to theater historian Jack Stewart, it was called the St. Charles Orpheum when it was a part of the Orpheum Circuit; then the Orpheum. Then, when the beautiful movie palace called the Orpheum opened on University Place, the name of the St. Charles Street theater was changed to the Shubert St. Charles, then later to the Saenger St. Charles, and finally to the St. Charles. (Changes of ownership by the three major theater companies were always reflected in the name.)

Standing on the bricked sidewalk in front of the Casino Theater on Rampart Street in 1920 were Mr. Pujol, owner; Arthur and Bertha Pigeon; Marcelle Pigeon, twelve; Miss Pujol, sister of Mr. Pujol and co-owner; a friend who sold tickets; and Eddie Pigeon, ten. Bertha was the author's great-aunt. She handled the candy concession. The theater was on the second floor. The building had formerly been the French Union Hall. Patrons sat on kitchen chairs. Balconies ran along the sides of the theater, and doors to balconies were left open for air.

The Orpheum opened on University Place in 1921, showing silent movies and vaudeville. It was one of the grand movie palaces of New Orleans.

THE THREE MAJOR MOVING PICTURE PALACES

The city's three movie palaces—the Saenger, the Loew's State, and the Orpheum—all opened in the twenties.

The Orpheum opened first, at 129 University Place in 1921. It was designed by architect G. Albert Lansburgh and local architect Samuel Stone. It was the city's best example of a "vertical" theater, with its two balconies and a loftlike seating area above the second balcony. It made the most effective use of stage space of any theater in town.

It was built as a vaudeville house, and big-time vaudeville acts were booked there like Harry Houdini and Burns and Allen. These acts came from New York nightclubs or rode the Keith-Orpheum circuit, leaping from Atlanta to New Orleans, playing a one-night stand, then moving on to Baton Rouge, Houston, or Dallas. The Orpheum was financed by Keith-Orpheum, a national entertainment firm that brought stars from the Palace in New York to theaters throughout the country. In 1928, Keith-Orpheum merged with radio interests to form RKO.

By 1925, vaudeville was being compromised by the public's increasing delight in motion pictures. The Orpheum showed silent films between its matinee and evening performances.

Asa Booksh, longtime manager of the Orpheum, remembered a weekly dance contest there in the twenties. "The Charleston was quite a thing in those days [the late twenties]," he said in a Dixie-Roto article in the 1970s. "Everyone who could dance was dancing the Charleston."

The Orpheum also opened its doors to private parties. The Carnival ball of the Mistick Krewe of Comus was held there from 1924 to 1929.

The Rampart Street entrance to the Saenger Theatre, which was still under construction in 1927. To the left, part of the Hotel La Salle still stands. To the right is Rubenstein's Ready-to-Wear. Cars were allowed to park up to the neutral ground on an angle. (Courtesy The Historic New Orleans Collection, acc. no. 1979.89.7474)

The Loew's State, at 1108 Canal, opened in 1926. Designed by Thomas Lamb, the theater boasted a lobby with a magnificent staircase. Every door to the inner auditorium was hung with heavy velvet draperies, and crystal sconces lined the walls of the massive carpeted staircases.

The Saenger, at Canal and North Rampart, across the street from the Loew's, opened in 1927. It was hailed as the "Florentine Palace of Splendor." "The day the Saenger opened, the city stopped cold," said Rene Brunet, Jr., moving picture entrepreneur and historian. "Parades passed, Mayor O'Keefe cut the ribbon to open the theater, and half the movie stars in Hollywood were here. The French consul attended the opening, as well as Mayor O'Keefe, the Boswell Sisters, and a full orchestra."

On Saturday, June 14, 1929, the movie *Evangeline*, starring Dolores Del Rio, premiered at the Saenger. The star came to New Orleans dressed in what was later called "Evangeline blue," and the store windows displayed dresses of that color.

The Saenger was designed by architect Emile Weil, who placed magnificent statuary atop walls beneath a ceiling that emulated a star-studded sky. The building is listed in the National Register of Historic Places as one of the outstanding movie palaces in predepression America. The first movie shown there was *Blonde or Brunette*, a comedy-farce of French married life.

PLUSH WAS THE WORD

In the movie palaces, patrons marveled at the opulence of the architecture and the formality of white-gloved, uniformed ushers and ticket-takers, and maids in attendance in the huge, mirrored rest rooms. "Plenty of good seating in the mezzanine," the ticket-takers called out. "Stairs to the right."

The city newspapers devoted a special section to a movie palace when it opened. The *Item* did this when the Loew's State opened.

NEIGHBORHOOD THEATERS

Scattered throughout the city were neighborhood theaters where the bill changed every night, and "special" movies were saved for Saturday and Sunday shows. In the neighborhood shows, no bill of fare was complete without news, a comedy, and, after talkies arrived, a chapter of a thriller serial.

THE MOVIES TALK!

In 1928, the Tudor Theater, owned by the Saenger Company, installed Vitaphone sound-reproducing equipment and showed the first sound picture in New Orleans, *The Glorious Betsy*, with Dolores Costello and Conrad Nagel. It ran for six weeks. This pushed the competition into sound movies.

The Orpheum showed sound movies and vaudeville for a while, beginning in 1928, but after the banks failed in 1929 and the depression set in in the early thirties, the theater dropped vaudeville and continued with movies only.

The Academy Awards were presented for the first time on May 16, 1929. It was the first and last time a silent film would ever win the statuette (not yet named). For the period of 1927-28, the movie *Wings*, starring Richard Arlen, "Buddy" Rogers, and Clara Bow, with a twenty-second appearance by Gary Cooper, took

Rudolph Valentino, silent screen idol, as "The Sheik of Arabi." Valentino visited New Orleans and danced the tango with his wife, Winifred Hudnut, on the stage of the Athenaeum Theater near Lee Circle in March 1923.

the prize. The following year, the talkie *Broadway Melody* won the award and talking pictures swept the boards. Sound brought a new element to screen art, and there were new categories to be judged and honored.

RIVALRY FOR THE TALKIES

With Al Jolson's *Jazz Singer* among the coming attractions at the Tudor Theater, the rival Loew's State Theater announced on August 1, 1928, that the installation of sound equipment would be complete within a few days. Loew's management said the change would allow its patrons "the perfect synchronization of sight and sound in a manner that is at once startlingly realistic and supremely entertaining." The Loew's first "talkie" was *The Loves of an Actress*, with Pola Negri, which opened August 18. Pola Negri's film career soon vanished along with silent films.

Another silent screen star who bit the dust when "talkies" arrived was John Gilbert, often paired with Greta Garbo as a romantic duo both on and off the silver screen. In *Flesh and the Devil*, the handsome, virile actor made the women in the audiences swoon with his passionate kisses and embraces, but they had a quick change of heart when they heard his high, effeminate voice.

The most famous of all silent screen stars, Rudolph Valentino, known best for his role in *The Sheik*, thrilled an audience at the old Athenaeum Theater on Lee Circle on March 29, 1923, when he and his wife, Winifred Hudnut, performed the tango, the dance he had made famous on the screen. Earlier that day, a crowd of hundreds had gathered at the old Union Station to meet Valentino, but he and his wife, dressed in heavy coats with their faces almost hidden, escaped their fans who had been waiting for hours. Valentino died in his twenties from a ruptured appendix.

The Athenaeum and the Shriners Temple, St. Charles Avenue near Lee Circle, in the twenties. Some Carnival balls were held in the Athenaeum, as well as other entertainment.

ORGANS SET THE MOOD

We cannot leave the movies of the twenties without some reference to those marvelous organs and organists who set the mood for the silent movie on screen. Mary NaDal Hoffman and her husband, Robert Hoffman, both "played their way" into the history of New Orleans silent movies while seated at an organ.

At that time, Bob Hoffman was the city's premier organist and composer, remembered chiefly for his song "I'm Alabama Bound." They were "in" from the beginning, and for them, the silent movies were a wide-open road.

Mary started her musical career playing piano in Woolworth in Memphis as a sheet music demonstrator, when a man introduced himself and asked if she would come to New Orleans and be the manager of the sheet music department in the biggest Kress store in the world. She took the job. She arrived in 1913 when ragtime was the rage.

At Kress, she met a West End band director who introduced her to Bob Hoffman, who had just returned from playing vaudeville in Alabama. He told Mary that the organ was the coming thing, and at an organ in a St. Charles Avenue church, he taught her what his music professor was teaching him. After four lessons, he told her of an opening at the Plaza Theater. She went down to see the manager and got the job.

They played seven days a week. Some theaters like the Strand and the Saenger had orchestras as well as organists. Some movies came with musical scores, but others provided cue sheets suggesting what was needed—chase music, hearts and flowers, a dirge, a wedding march. Sometimes the organist just improvised.

Mary grew tired of moving from town to town with the Saenger group and retired. Bob married and was widowed but continued playing the organ until "talkies" left him unemployed in 1932. Mary and Bob met once again and married late in life.

According to Rene Brunet, moving picture historian, the Robert Martin Wonder Organ at the Saenger Theatre is the original, dating back to 1927. Recently, Brunet, an accomplished organist, played the instrument. The organ at the Loew's was not used after 1932, he says, although it remained in the theater for a long time before it was removed.

Father Edward Cummings, S.J., president of Loyola, spoke the first words over radio in Louisiana on Friday, March 31, 1922, the same day the license for WWL was granted by Washington. The telephone-like apparatus was located in Marquette Hall at Loyola. (Courtesy Father Thomas Clancy, S.J., and Loyola University)

CHAPTER SEVEN

Radio: Daddy Built
a Crystal Set

I don't go out late; no place to go, I'm home about eight:
just me an' my radio. . . .

MARCONI SENT RADIO WAVES through the air in 1895, but it was not until November 2, 1920 that the first licensed commercial station, KDKA in Pittsburgh, broadcast the returns of the Harding-Cox election, the first great national event in broadcast history.

Radio historians disagree about which station came first. Some did primitive broadcasts as early as 1909. But if the criteria are that a station do continuous programming and be licensed by the federal government, then Pittsburgh's KDKA was first.

EARLY RADIO STATIONS OF NEW ORLEANS

The first radio station to broadcast in Louisiana was WWL, which sent out radio waves from Marquette Hall at Loyola University in New Orleans on March 31, 1922. Ten days earlier, on March 21, WGV, a joint venture of the Interstate Electric Company and the New Orleans *Item*, was licensed to broadcast by the Commerce Department, but it missed its chance to be first on the air by spending time perfecting arrangements with distant points.

When Loyola University got its license for WWL, the Jesuits, sensing the history-making value of being first, did not wait even a single day. Father Edward Cummings, S.J., president of the university, seated himself in front of the trunk set's telephone-style microphone at 10:52 A.M. and began the history of Louisiana broadcasting. He started with a commercial (what else?), an announcement of a major campaign to raise $1,500,000 to build six new campus buildings at Loyola. This was followed by a piano composition by Giuseppe Ferrate of the Newcomb College faculty and a statement about the station's prospects by Edward Cassidy.

After the program, a telephone call to the Immaculate Conception College on Baronne and Common determined that the program had been heard, received on a "catwhisker" crystal set. Few others besides the Jesuits had heard it since it was unannounced and broadcast during the morning when men were at work.

87

Evening programs followed carrying the campaign message, but offering cornet, piano, and tenor solos, and a recording of the Edison Concert Band.

This was not the beginning of radio involvement at Loyola. Father Anton L. Kunkel, S.J., had found himself drawn to the work being done in wireless telegraphy throughout the previous decade. With Father Biever, he'd bought $150 worth of radio parts and set up a receiving set and a transmitter, receiving help from Joe du Triel, a wireless operator. During World War I, the armed forces had taken over all radio facilities for training purposes, but when the war was over, veterans who wanted radio careers came to classes at Loyola, which by then was called the Radio School.

Edward T. Cassidy, a seminarian-physicist, headed the school, together with Joe du Triel, now the assistant superintendent of American Marconi's Gulf Division, and field inspector of the Radio Service Section's New Orleans District Office. On a ship docked in port, they found a discarded Morse code transmitter with huge coils, Leyden jar condensers, and vacuum tubes, all contained in a trunk. They bought it, modified it, and built their own voice modulator. When completed, the equipment supported a microphone extending from the trunk set on a long arched arm, much like telephones in use at the time. An antenna wire was strung from Marquette Hall to the steeple of Holy Name Church. A Department of Commerce authorization was requested.

In 1922, such applications were filed with the nearest district office of the Radio Service, which then forwarded them to Washington for approval. Headquarters for eight states including Louisiana was in the Customs House. When Loyola's approval was received on March 31, it stipulated broadcasting could be done on a wavelength of 833 kilocycles with a transmitter of 100 watts.

WWL's call letters had belonged to the Pacific Mail Steamship Company's steamer, *San Jose*, which ran aground in August 1921 and could not be refloated. Its radio call letters were put back into the lot of available letters, where Loyola got them through the "luck of the draw." The letters had no special meaning to the university.

WHAT WAS A RADIO GOOD FOR?

Although none could deny the miracle of sound being transmitted and received over long distances, *without wires*, people could not imagine any practical use the radio would serve, not even as entertainment, in the beginning. It was hard to imagine that people would have nothing better to do than sit around listening to someone read a recipe for pralines or sing "Ah, Sweet Mystery of Life." Even vaudeville held little appeal when not seen.

Radio was actually a distraction. People couldn't hear each other talk with the radio on. The only ones it seemed to benefit were shut-ins, the elderly, and the feebleminded. As time went on, however, audiences grew. More and more radios were bought.

With no precedent to go by, neither station managers nor listeners could project that in time everyone would depend on radio for instant news of the city, state, and nation; weather forecasts; baseball and football games; results of local, state, and national elections; music; drama; lectures; concerts; and religious services.

Firsts were the order of the day in the spring of 1922: the first children's program, the first radio drama, the first "remote control" broadcast, and the first amateur-night talent contest (the winners were Martha and Connie Boswell, whose later fame would take them far beyond the city of New Orleans).

On April 5, the Commerce Department licensed Tulane University's wireless telephone operation and designated it WAAC.

In May 1922, the magazine *Radio Broadcast* printed its first issue, concerning itself mostly with how a radio station could finance itself. Early broadcasters were not in radio for direct profit. They were in it for one of four reasons: to promote the sale of radios (Interstate Electric), to call attention to the business that owned the station (Uhalt), to increase newspaper circulation (the newspaper stations; by 1922, seventy publishers in the country had secured permission to go on the air), and to educate or evangelize.

A RACE TO THE AIRWAVES AMONG
THE NEWSPAPER DAILIES

A race followed among the three newspaper dailies to get a radio station on the air. The *Times-Picayune* transmitter would be located in the home of Val Jensen, an auto salesman who lived on St. Patrick Street. The call letters were to be WAAB. For the *New Orleans States*, the transmitter was installed in the home of Clyde Randall, and licensed in his name and that of the *States*.

On April 6, the *Item*-Interstate Electric (which was licensed before WWL) announced its intentions of opening shortly. The *Times-Picayune* announced its intentions of beating them. The race was on. Musicians were borrowed from the Strand Theater, a switch was thrown, two lamps glowed red in front of the instrument panel, and WGV (*Item*) was on the air. The *Times-Picayune*'s WAAB debuted later that same evening with a recording by Enrico Caruso obtained from Werlein's Music Store.

Half the stations that had applied for licenses in Louisiana by 1924 closed down for three reasons: high start-up costs, high operating expenses, and lack of income. University stations fared best since the stations were set up in university buildings, were on the air for short periods of time, and were manned by volunteers. The *Times-Picayune* finally abandoned its radio station, and the other newspaper dailies did the same.

WDSU BEGINS BROADCASTING

In 1923 the call letters WCBE were assigned to the Uhalt Radio Company, a partnership of two brothers, William and Joseph Uhalt, the latter a twenty-three-year-old genius of early commercial radio. In later years Uhalt would cite July 1923 as the starting date, but Commerce Department records show 1924. The two brothers, who had served as wireless operators aboard ship, opened a radio shop on Baronne Street in the early 1920s. Joe was self-educated, an avid reader, and articulate in many subjects. His career in radio spanned two decades.

In 1927, WCBE underwent changes. The older brother, William, dropped out. Joe carried on, moving to the top floor of the DeSoto Hotel. He established a relationship with the *New Orleans States* for remote broadcasts, and in July 1928, the station's call letters were changed to WDSU. *W* indicated that it was east of the Mississippi, *D* stood for DeSoto, *S* for *States*, and *U* for Uhalt.

WSMB GOES ON THE AIR

In April 1925, WSMB went into business as a joint venture of the Saenger Company and the Maison Blanche Company, which accounts for the call letters. This was the first professional (Class B) station in New Orleans. The Maison Blanche Building would provide the studio space; the Saenger would supply the talent from the pool of singers, musicians, and vaudeville acts in its many theaters. The signal was transmitted between two towers on top of the Maison Blanche Building. With broadcast power of 500 watts, it was the city's strongest station. In 1925, it was broadcasting a continuous schedule of seventeen hours a day.

Because radio was a new concept in the twenties, station managers had a hard time finding a format that would appeal to listeners. At first, WSMB broadcast a series of live performances from the studio, as well as recordings. One broadcast featured an orchestra of thirty musicians jammed into the studio, playing live. Vaudeville was broadcast either from the studio or from the Saenger Theatre via telephone lines.

WSMB, owned jointly by the Saenger Company and Maison Blanche (hence the call letters), was on the top floor of the Maison Blanche Building. Its transmitters were atop the building (1925).

Canal Street looking toward the river, 1927. At left is the Southern Railway Terminal, Saenger Theatre (where the Hotel La Salle had been), and, beyond, two transmitters of WSMB atop the Maison Blanche Building. At right is Loew's State Theater.

CANAL STREET, LOOKING EAST, NEW ORLEANS, LA.—5

WJBW was licensed in 1926 to Charles C. Carlson, a self-employed electrician who used his home for a studio. The station remained a small, independent enterprise until 1949.

By 1929, WJBO was on the air. Its letters indicate an affiliation with the Orpheum, but the 1929 telephone directory shows it broadcasting from the Roosevelt Hotel. Victor Schiro, later mayor of New Orleans, was a disc jockey on that station.

NETWORK BROADCASTING

By the Radio Act of 1927, Congress established a Federal Radio Commission to control radio broadcasts. The Federal Communications Commission replaced it in 1934. The FCC licenses broadcasters, assigns frequencies, designates call letters, and controls station power.

A network was defined by the Federal Radio Commission as "the simultaneous broadcast of an identical program by two or more connected stations." By the summer of 1927, NBC had two different chains carrying programs: a "Red" network of fifteen stations, and a "Blue" network of ten stations. Another eight stations were affiliated with both chains. In September 1927, NBC found itself in competition with CBS. Network broadcasting had come to stay.

By spring 1929, nine stations remained on the air in Louisiana, five of them in New Orleans. Classified as commercial stations in New Orleans were WDSU (a CBS affiliate), WSMB (an NBC affiliate), and WJBO. All were offering time to advertisers.

WWL GOES COMMERCIAL

When WWL embarked on a policy of commercial radio in 1929, it did so with the stipulation that it would operate on a nonprofit basis, all revenues over and above operating expenses being channeled into the university's treasury. Jean Pasquet, a musician who had previously volunteered his time to the station, was now hired as program director, announcer, and sales manager, all for $150 a month, with no provision for commissions on new accounts. Rates for advertising were now shown on a national rate card.

By 1929, WWL was an independent clear channel station of 500 watts' broadcasting power. One hour's time sold for $150. If the "spot" ran for one hour, once a week for thirteen weeks, the rate per hour was $142.50; and so the rates were reduced according to frequency on the air.

AIR TIME, A STRANGE NEW COMMODITY

In the beginning, there was a general reluctance to use radio as an advertising medium, strange as that may seem today. People in high places expressed hostility to the idea. Newspapers printed editorials asking if such a gift from God should be used to peddle soap. Critics compared it to medicine shows.

But radio stations were expensive to run. The station had to rent space for a studio, buy equipment for transmitting, and, in time, pay good prices for talent and writers. Selling radio time was the logical solution.

But what were they selling? The answer was "air time," a strange new commodity that no one could see or hold in his hand, but one that businesses were willing to pay big money for. Then, too, if someone sold a station to someone else, what was *he* selling? The answer was the license, the space on the spectrum. How odd! It was just sound passing through air. Who would buy it? The answer was: lots of people, for a great deal of money.

Advertisers were discovering that radio was an effective means of selling products. And once paid advertising began, there was a tidal wave of money being thrown at the stations.

It came to be an accepted fact that if you were in retail sales and you advertised on radio, your sales tripled; if you did not, you could close your doors. The sale of radios rose from less than 2 million in 1920 to 600 million in 1929. By then, 618 radio stations were in business across the country, and networks were broadcasting regularly from coast to coast.

In March 1924, it was estimated that the average New Orleanian spent $100 for an assembled receiving set, though many were still buying parts and building sets at home. The 1923 City Directory listed five shops selling radio supplies; the 1925 directory listed seventeen.

WWL IN 1929

In 1929, WWL was still only a local radio station denied full radio time by the Federal Radio Commission. Not until 1934 was it granted "full-time" status. Later, in 1940, it became a 50,000-watt clear channel station, one of only forty in the country.

New program features were added in 1929, such as dance music from the Restaurant de la Louisiane. "Amos 'n' Andy," already a national phenomenon, had local copies. WWL called it "Smoky Joe and Tee Tain." The *Times-Picayune* radio listings of June 19, 1929 show it broadcast on WDSU as "Smoky Joe and Cinders."

DADDY MAKES A CRYSTAL SET

In 1921, my father was twenty-one. Intelligent and curious about new inventions, and very adept with his hands, he bought the makings of a crystal set, which could be purchased at any hobby shop. He then followed the directions given in the newspaper as to how to put it together. Using an empty Quaker Oats box about three inches in diameter as his cylinder, he built a radio set.

Instructions for assembling the tuning coil, the cylinder, the base, the tuner, the ground wire, the earphone, the antenna, and the crystal diode seem so complicated that you wonder how anyone ever succeeded at putting them together. But my father did. He said he didn't care what was being broadcast. He was happy to get any signals at all. To him, it was a miracle.

To me it would have been a miracle if I'd been able to put it together. I am one of the thousands who do not know how to set the time for taping a program on my VCR when I'm out. My father was a bit inventive, however, and he was a very patient man. His crystal set worked.

In the early twenties, the first radio programs were heard over earphones. By 1923, loudspeakers, like huge horns, replaced earphones. Aerials (antennas) were still outside the house. By the 1930s, aerials and loudspeakers were built into radios. By that time, programs were reaching millions.

A shopper listens through earphones. The number of radio-owning families nationwide was 60,000 in 1922 and 13,750,000 in 1930.

AN HISTORICAL RADIO BLOOPER

Our late congressman F. Edward Hebert wrote in his autobiography, *The Last of the Titans,* that he took a job handling public relations for Loyola in the twenties. This job included sports publicity, and that meant broadcasting football games over the radio.

"Eddie" Hebert and Bill Coker, a well-known New Orleanian, announced the first football game broadcast over WWL. The star of the Loyola team at that time was Elton ("Bucky") Moore, who had been dubbed "The Dixie Flyer." A fine halfback with an elusive hip movement, Bucky was given the ball on the ten-yard line. He broke around his own right end and headed for the goal line.

Coker was at the mike. "Moore's got the ball. He's off the wide right end and cuts in. There he goes. He passes the twenty, the thirty, the forty—*look at that son of a bitch go!"* Coker screamed into the mike of the Jesuit-owned station. Coker and Hebert suppressed their laughter, but the faux pas went down in the history of radio bloopers.

Some national network programs being broadcast in New Orleans in the twenties were Paul Whiteman and His Orchestra; the voices of Jessica Dragonette, Lannie Ross, and Morton Downey; and the Radio Town Crier, with Alexander Woolcott.

Not until the thirties was the cream coming to the top in radio entertainment, talent, and format. Now listeners were becoming addicted to it. Fibber McGee and Molly, Kate Smith, Eddie Cantor, Burns and Allen, Jack Benny, and Charlie McCarthy and Edgar Bergen were household words.

It would be hard to imagine what people would have done during the depression without their radios for company and entertainment. Movies also chased away the blues, but radio, after the initial investment, was free. And how we all loved it!

Rudy Vallee and Graham McNamee were on for Fleischmann's Yeast. People in New Orleans were interested in national programming, and everyone knew Rudy Vallee.

Helen Marie Abadie was the lady chosen to "sponsor" this beautiful 1922 Auburn Touring Car when the automobile dealers of New Orleans displayed their new 1922 models at Audubon Park and took prospective buyers for a ride. (Courtesy Bill Gallmann, Jr.)

CHAPTER EIGHT

Cars, Streetcars, Trains, Boats, and Planes

Won't you come with me, Lucille,
In my merry Oldsmobile?

W‍HEN WE PICTURE THE STREETS of New Orleans in the twenties, especially the areas where traffic was heaviest, we must remember that horse-drawn vehicles equaled, if not outnumbered, cars. The fact that automobiles had been manufactured since 1899, when the Detroit Automobile Company made Henry Ford its chief engineer, did not mean that everyone had the money or the desire to own a car. Many were afraid the contraptions would explode or catch fire or just "go dead," leaving them stranded far from home.

The transition from horse-drawn vehicles to cars took many decades, and the twenties was the decade caught right in the middle of that change. Even as late as the thirties, horse-drawn carriages could be seen on the city's streets. In the forties, two elderly ladies who lived on Prytania Street had their liveried servant take out the horse-drawn hansom cab every afternoon to take them for a ride. Also, on St. Charles Avenue, a well-to-do family kept their own stable on the grounds for housing their carriage and horses.

It was the dynamic Henry Ford who put cars on the road, and made them affordable for the largest number of people at the lowest possible price. In 1908, in his own company, he was producing Model Ts, making young men salivate. With his "assembly-line" method of organization, he made his plant the largest motor company in the world.

THE GOLDEN AGE OF THE AUTOMOBILE

When car buying finally took hold, it created a revolution in American life. It changed family habits, allowing the family an outing in the fresh air to more distant places, like West End Park or Spanish Fort Amusement Park on the lakefront. "Taking a ride in the machine" was an end in itself, not a matter of getting from one place to another. It allowed French Quarter dwellers or residents of the Garden District to work in the Central Business District and commute back and forth each day.

Of course, many still commuted by streetcar, as they always had, but owning an automobile was a mark of success. The growing number of cars in the city brought

95

In 1920, a motoring party stops in a park for a picture. L to R: Grace Ton and author's father, Earl Schultis, sitting on running board. At wheel, Earl's sister Hazel. Standing, her current beau, Everett Newman. The car belonged to Everett.

about the development of the suburbs, especially Lakeview, Gentilly, and Metairie. It gave Orleanians a new freedom, but since most cars were bought on the installment plan, it saddled the family with debt.

EASY PAYMENT PLAN

"Paying on time" eventually became a way of life that enabled Orleanians to own not only cars, but homes and new appliances as they came on the market. Owning a car was something most people would not have been able to do without the installment plan.

The automobile became America's leading industry. It was the largest customer for steel, lead, rubber, nickel, and gasoline. One dollar out of every five that consumers spent in the twenties went for automobiles and their upkeep.

Cars became part of the American dream. F. Scott Fitzgerald put them in his books, and the workingman adored them. They changed his courting and travel habits. Suddenly, he could go anywhere until he came to water, and even then, his car could be taken aboard ferries.

In 1920, hydraulic brakes were added, and in 1922, balloon tires. The car became more attractive each year, with rakish fenders, vibrant colors, eye-catching hood ornaments, tilted windshields, and comfortable upholstery.

In New Orleans in 1920, cars were still somewhat of a luxury, but would come into more general use as the decade progressed. When a young man like my father saved enough money to buy a car, or bought one on time, he became the envy of the neighborhood. His friends gathered around it to inspect its wonders. My father drove to his *parrain*'s house and to Aunt Onieda's to "show them the car." He had his picture taken sitting behind the wheel, standing beside the car, and with friends inside the car. His automobile was his treasure.

In 1920, author's father, twenty, sits proudly at the wheel of his own car.

Frank R. Marfese at the wheel of the Studebaker, five-year-old Maude Marfese, and Grandmother Marfese, who was picture shy. When it rained, isinglass shields had to be snapped on. This would cause a greenhouse effect. By the time you finally got them on, the rain stopped and you'd be wetter from perspiration than from the rain. (Courtesy Maude Puissegur)

Eleonora O'Keefe, with baby Arthur J. III, sits on the running board of the family car, a Reo. The license plate shows 1925. In 1926, Mrs. O'Keefe's father-in-law would become mayor of New Orleans on the death of Martin Behrman. (Courtesy the late Eleonora O'Keefe)

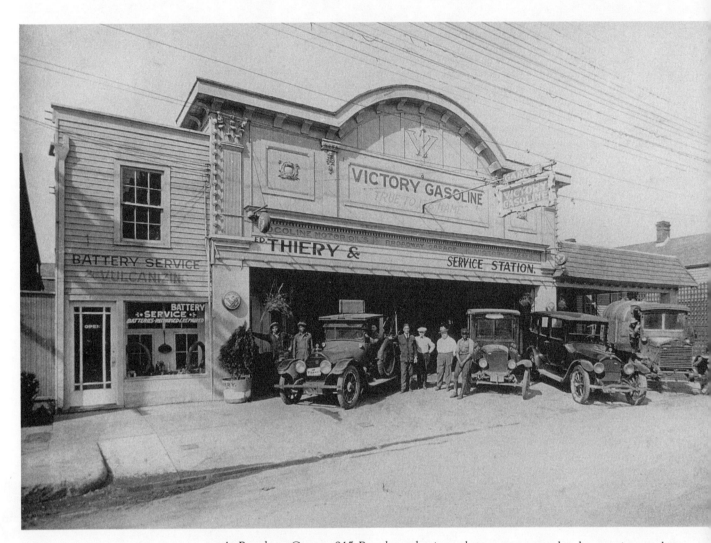

At Broadway Garage, 915 Broad, mechanics and customers stopped to have a picture taken, 1925. (Courtesy Earl K. Long Library, UNO)

The pride of any family was its car. Here's a beauty with tilted windshield, hood ornament, and wood-spoke, noninflated tires, 1927. (Courtesy Judy Pesses)

A sailor suit was what fourteen-year-old Philip La Valle wore in 1927 when he served curb service at Jake Oronato's Ice Cream Parlor at 5555 Canal Blvd. When the government decreed that civilians were not to wear navy uniforms, La Valle had to change his costume. The car is a Model-A Ford; the driver is Charles Coscino, Oronato's son-in-law. The site of the ice-cream parlor is today's Plantation Coffee House. (Courtesy Philip La Valle)

Albert Bianchini, with a foot on the running board of his Ford, 1927. (Courtesy Judy Pesses)

Philip La Valle (in the white suit) poses with his 1929 Hupmobile Strait-Eight sedan. The year was 1931, and La Valle was a carhop at Lenfant's on Canal Boulevard earning ninety dollars a month plus tips—not bad during the depression. (Courtesy Philip La Valle)

A salesman tries to peddle his product, FAC-TRY-LYK, with which you could paint your car as professionally as the factory. He stands before a United Cigar Store. (Courtesy Earl K. Long Library, UNO)

NEW ORLEANS TO CHICAGO IN 1927

In the 1920s, Americans were taking to the road in large numbers. More cars meant new roads, uniform road signs, billboards, road maps, and campsites of varying quality.

In 1927, my mother and father, their two small children, and my grandmother took a trip in their Chevrolet touring car from New Orleans to Chicago, quite a distance what with the cars and roads of the time. Stopping at tourist camps was mandatory, since these were the least expensive accommodations. Even with babies, they made do with community camp showers, washbasins, and toilets, and enjoyed a wonderful adventure without complaint. They were young. Being able to venture so far from home and see the countryside and the skyscrapers of a big city opened up a whole new world to them.

FILLING STATIONS SOLD GROCERIES

Filling stations mushroomed around the country, and indeed, around New Orleans. With an eye for business, the station owner sometimes "carried" bread, sandwich makings, fruit, and other mainstays for the traveler, or rented out space to a grocer. Lunchrooms sprang up around the stations, and sometimes, little shopping centers, forerunners of later suburban shopping areas, appeared along the highway. If a tourist stopped at one of these, he was likely to be approached by one or more vendors.

The automobile had created a number of new and thriving industries that were to grow and prosper in the twenties, until the crash and the depression snuffed them out.

THE STREETCARS OF NEW ORLEANS

The electric streetcar played the most dramatic role in the development and growth of New Orleans in the nineteenth and early twentieth centuries. It was not a coincidence that Lafayette City (today's Garden District) became incorporated in 1833, the very same year that the first railroad, the New Orleans and Carrollton Railroad Company (today the St. Charles Streetcar), was incorporated by the Louisiana legislature.

As the city became overcrowded, people moved to the newer areas, Lafayette City, Jefferson City, and Carrollton City, all served by the N.O. and Carrollton Railroad. The earliest developments were close to the railroad line, for swift and easy transportation to work, shopping, amusements, and visiting.

By the turn of the century, so many streetcars converged upon Canal Street (which was included in every route except the Napoleon Line) that it was necessary to remove the Henry Clay Statue. It had stood for years in the middle of the neutral ground on Canal Street at the corner of St. Charles. It had become an obstacle to streetcar traffic.

THE 1923 PERLEY A. THOMAS STREETCAR

The streetcar model in use after 1923 is the same one we see today on the St. Charles Streetcar line, the only remaining line in the city from that time. It was designed and built by the Perley A. Thomas Car Company of High Point, North Carolina.

Looking down St. Charles Avenue from Poydras, 1920. Note the streetcar's "cowcatcher," laundry hanging on a wrought-iron balcony, and the fortresslike Masonic Temple Building on the corner of St. Charles and Perdido (replaced in 1926 by the present Masonic Temple). At right is the St. Charles Orpheum, at 432 St. Charles. Its name was changed in 1921 when the new Orpheum was built on University Place. (Photo by Charles L. Franck, courtesy Ken and Lynn Cheskin for the late Abe Oppenheim)

In New Orleans, it is called a streetcar, not a trolley, and it is treasured by the city. Over the years, improvements have included replacement of the mahogany sash and canvas roof with metal. Today, exact-change fare boxes and automatic metal doors have made the vehicle operable by one person. This was not so at the turn of the century, when my grandfather Pigeon was a streetcar conductor on the St. Charles line and it took two men to run a streetcar, one driving the vehicle in front, the other collecting fares and giving change at the rear.

The most nostalgic features of the 1923 streetcar are the exposed ceiling light-bulbs and the rich wooden seats with their fine brass handholds on the aisle corners. The seats can be reversed, depending on the direction the streetcar is going.

Even though many families bought cars in the twenties, the most common mode of transportation was still by streetcar, especially when going to work. An automobile was treasured and not left on the street all day at the mercy of the elements. Parking lots were few.

RAILROADS

Between 1865 and 1945, New Orleans became a railroad center almost in spite of herself. Situated at the junction of the Mississippi and the Gulf, she had the

Alfred Pigeon, author's maternal grand-father, in his uniform as a streetcar conductor, 1921.

The value of coffee far exceeded that of any other import in New Orleans in the twenties (over $32,500,000 a year). British lines brought most of the coffee from Brazil, then took on cargoes for European ports, and there got cargoes for Brazil and Argentina, making a triangular run. This was a New Orleans warehouse for coffee on the riverfront.

advantage of shipping, by boat and by rail, not only the products of the agricultural South, but of Latin America as well. Latin America provided two products much in demand: coffee and bananas. New Orleans became a prime port of entry and distribution for both. The value of coffee far exceeded that of any other import. New Orleans in the twenties was the second largest port in the United States, outranked only by New York in the matter of tonnage.

The Union Station (1893) on Howard Avenue and Rampart Street (site of today's Union Passenger Terminal) served as the New Orleans terminal for the Illinois Central Railroad. I.C. tracks ran from New Orleans to Chicago and out to the Pacific Northwest. This was the largest of the five stations scattered around the city and used by nine different railroad companies in the twenties. It would be three more decades before they would be consolidated into one. Into this station also came the Yazoo and Mississippi Valley and the Southern Pacific trains.

The Southern Railway Terminal Station (1908) was at the corner of Canal and Basin streets, facing Elks Place. On the river side of the terminal was the Hotel La Salle (the Saenger Theatre would be built there in 1927); on the lake side, Krauss Department Store (1903). From the Southern Terminal, over the years, New Orleanians traveled to New York on the Southerner, an all-reserved streamliner; the Crescent, an all-Pullman train; the Piedmont Limited; and the Pelican.

The second most important product imported from Central America in the twenties was bananas. Here is a freight car of the Illinois Central Railroad on the riverfront in which they will be transported. (Courtesy Earl K. Long Library, UNO)

The Union Passenger Terminal at Howard Avenue and Rampart Street for the Illinois Central, Yazoo and Mississippi Valley, Southern Pacific, and Gulf Coast lines.

The Southern Railway Terminal Station on Canal and Basin streets opened in 1908 and shut down in 1954. The Southerner tracks ran from New Orleans to New York.

The Trans-Mississippi Passenger Station on Annunciation and Thalia was constructed in 1916. Railways of the Texas Pacific-Missouri Pacific used this terminal. It was one of five depots abandoned in 1954 when the new Union Passenger Terminal opened. It was demolished in 1964, the last of the five buildings to go.

Six ferry crossings in or near New Orleans allowed ferries to transport cars and passengers from the city to Algiers, Gretna, and Westwego on the West Bank of the river.

The Louisville and Nashville Station (1901), at Canal Street and the river, was in use for fifty years. The L&N tracks ran from New Orleans all along the Gulf Coast and north to the Ohio River Valley. The Pontchartrain line, which ran for the last time in 1932, sent its trains into the L&N Station in the twenties, instead of making its terminus at the end of Elysian Fields Avenue. The L&N ran under the pedestrian up-ramp for the Algiers Ferry, making the area one of heavy traffic.

The handsomest of the railroad stations in the twenties was the Trans-Mississippi Passenger Station (1916), at Annunciation and Thalia. The Texas-Pacific and Missouri-Pacific tracks ran from this terminal.

The fifth and last station was the Louisiana and Arkansas (1923), a Kansas City Southern station, on Rampart Street.

FERRIES

In the twenties, the First District ferry crossed from the foot of Canal Street to Algiers; the Third, from the foot of Esplanade Avenue to Algiers; the Fourth, from Jackson Avenue to Gretna; the Sixth, from Louisiana Avenue to the Harvey Canal; the Richard Street ferry, from Richard Street to Freetown; and the Walnut Street ferry, from Walnut Street to Westwego. Early twentieth-century New Orleans ferries were twin-hulled catamaran-type vessels, driven by a recessed paddle wheel.

A leisurely ride on a riverboat on a Sunday afternoon is taken by Carmen and Ed Villere and Carmen's brother Rene Pigeon, 1921. The lady in profile between the men is Marie Caro, the author's grandmother. The lady at right, half-shown, is the author's mother.

One of the most picturesque sections of the New Orleans levee was the landing place of the oyster luggers, which brought oysters from the lower coast of Louisiana to New Orleans. In the 1920s, sailboats gave way to motor-powered vessels.

One New Orleans ferry with an interesting background was the *Gouldsboro*, built in 1863 as a federal ship in the Civil War and initially named *Chickasaw*. After the war, it was sold at auction, stripped, and served for a time as a barge. In 1880, it was converted into a rail ferry. All during the twenties, and until the Huey P. Long Bridge was built in 1935, trains were ferried across the Mississippi. Mules were used to haul the twenty-ton freight cars on and off the ferry transfer boats.

Until 1958, all the ferryboats were privately owned. One owner, Thomas Pickles, once held the entire ferry franchise in New Orleans. When the Greater New Orleans Mississippi River Bridge was completed in 1958, however, all the ferries were shut down except for the Algiers and the Jackson, which were bought out by the Mississippi River Bridge Authority. Today, there are ferry crossings at Canal Street, Jackson Avenue, and Chalmette.

THE INDUSTRIAL CANAL
AND THE FIVE-MILE BRIDGE

The Inner Harbor Navigation Canal (the Industrial Canal), completed in April 1921, was the realization of the age-old dream of connecting the Mississippi River with Lake Pontchartrain. Built at a cost of $19 million, it provided industrial sites on deep water. It was dedicated May 5, 1921.

On February 6, 1923, the tugboat *Samson* chugged from the foot of Canal Street to the Industrial Canal lock. The water was then lowered six feet from the level of the river to the level of the lake, which took ten minutes. Governor Parker, Mayor Andrew McShane, and Dock Board officials were aboard the *Samson*.

The Navigation Canal (called the Industrial Canal) connected the Mississippi River with Lake Pontchartrain and gave New Orleans a big addition to her harbor facilities. It was dedicated, as shown here, on May 5, 1921.

The Five-Mile Bridge, also known as the Watson Bridge, across Lake Pontchartrain, was a toll bridge in 1928.

In 1928, the Five-Mile Bridge, also known as the Watson Bridge, was completed, crossing Lake Pontchartrain where I-10 East now crosses the lake on the Twin Spans. This bridge was part of the Old Spanish Trail from Palm Beach, Florida to Los Angeles, California. After Huey P. Long built "free" bridges along Highway 90 over Chef Menteur and the Rigolets, this toll bridge was out of business.

AVIATION IN THE TWENTIES

There was not a single airport in New Orleans in the 1920s. If a plane flew over, it was such a novelty that every boy in the neighborhood shielded his eyes and yelled up to the pilot, who was usually flying low enough to yell back from his open-air cockpit.

Planes took off and landed in cow pastures around the city and in City Park and Audubon Park. One such field was in the Jefferson Avenue-Claiborne section, which was open country then. Another, on St. Bernard Highway, was called Menefee Field. In 1926, Alvin Callender Field was constructed at Belle Chasse, six miles from New Orleans. It was named for Capt. Alvin Callender, who had been killed in World War I after shooting down fourteen German planes. Operations began there in 1928.

My husband, Al, tells a story about being called by his older brother to "come see something" when he was about six or seven years old (roughly 1930). They were then living on Pontchartrain Boulevard near Carrollton. The building his older brother had discovered was near the intersection of Carrollton and the New Basin Canal. It was nothing more than a big barn, but his brother had looked through a hole in the wooden wall and caught his breath. When Al peeked, he gasped at the sight. There, spread out before him, were six or seven fighter planes from the Great War. (It was not yet called World War I.)

To the two brothers, it was like a dream, seeing these beautiful flying machines that the "aces" had piloted in the war, kept there for lack of a better place as "war surplus." World War I was the first war in which planes had been used as fighting machines.

In civilian life after the war, passengers took the place of bombs. People living in Europe considered it "trendy" to fly across the English Channel in the early twenties. Air shows and barnstorming in the new flying machines were the rage.

New Orleanians saw their first flight exhibition in 1910 at the City Park Race Track, which was no longer used for racing. French aviator Louis Paulhan thrilled a crowd of 30,000 with his dips and dives and daring climbs. He actually took his biplane to an altitude of 600 feet above the grandstand. They called him the "Birdman."

John B. Moisant, twenty-seven, a native of Kankakee, Illinois, came to City Park and put on a show that included an attempt to break the altitude record (he failed) and a race with an automobile (he failed). In his next attempt to win $4,000 and the Michelin Cup for sustained flight (the record was 362.66 miles), he flew from City Park to a field near Harahan, where his flight would begin. In trying to land, his plane struck an air pocket a few feet from the ground. Moisant was catapulted from the plane and struck the ground, sustaining fatal injuries. New Orleans honored his memory by giving his name to the airport near Kenner. Moisant Airfield later became New Orleans International Airport.

In 1912, George Mestach carried thirty-two pounds of mail from New Orleans

Daily airmail service between New Orleans and Pilot Town, at the mouth of the river, began April 9, 1923. This is one of the flying boats of the New Orleans Air Line, started by Arthur Cambas. (Courtesy Lloyd W. Huber for the late Leonard V. Huber)

to Baton Rouge in his plane in one hour and thirty minutes. Daily airmail service between New Orleans and Pilot Town began in 1923. Arthur Cambas, who started the line, was awarded New Orleans' first airmail franchise by the post office department.

Another pioneer in the field was James R. Wedell, an aviation genius and pilot who put Louisiana on the map with his fleet, self-designed planes. Born in Texas City, Texas in 1900, he was a ninth-grade dropout, but he was a genius when it came to motors and machines. He bought two old planes before he knew how to fly, got them into shape for flying, and gave one to an aviator in exchange for flying lessons. In the twenties, he became a protégé of New Orleans millionaire Harry P. Williams, with whom he formed the Wedell-Williams Air Service Inc., and built and raced four revolutionary planes that set world speed records. Plane accidents within two years (1934-36) took his life, the life of his brother Walter, and his backer, Harry Williams. Wedell-Williams had received a contract to build fifty of their fast pursuit planes for the U.S. Army. The order was never filled.

Wedell was known for his many humanitarian efforts, such as searching in his plane for lost hunters or fishermen, or rushing people across the country to hospitals for emergency treatment.

An eagle monument dedicated to him now stands on the neutral ground of Canal Boulevard facing City Park Avenue.

James R. Wedell, aviation genius, designed and built fast pursuit planes. (Courtesy Lloyd W. Huber for the late Leonard V. Huber)

LUCKY LINDY, AN OVERNIGHT HERO

It was not until the daring flight of twenty-five-year-old Charles Lindbergh from New York to Paris that anyone began to take aviation seriously. Lindbergh, with his solo flight across the ocean, a feat which six pilots had died trying to accomplish, became the most famous figure of his time. On May 20, 1927, he flew his single engine plane, the *Spirit of St. Louis*, out over the Atlantic, with a

Harry P. Williams, the wealthy New Orleans backer of the Wedell brothers. (Courtesy Lloyd W. Huber for the late Leonard V. Huber)

111

Mayor Arthur O'Keefe holds an umbrella to protect Charles Lindbergh, the hero who made the first nonstop trans-Atlantic flight from New York to Paris in 1927. Lindbergh was welcomed to the city in a ticker-tape parade. (Courtesy Times-Picayune Publishing Company)

compass, five quarts of water, and five sandwiches, but no radio. Thirty-three and a half hours later, he landed at Le Bourget airfield. He had landed where he'd said he would, flying by the seat of his pants, and aviation was born.

He toured the country after that, a hero, feted and cheered in ticker-tape parades. Here in New Orleans, Mayor O'Keefe gave him the key to the city and accompanied him in his parade down Canal Street.

It was not until 1934 that our first airport, Shushan Airport (now New Orleans Airport), was completed on a man-made island at a cost of $4.5 million.

Pelicans
1923

MATTISON, P. BOGART, O.F. GILBERT, Manager TUCKER, O.F.

THOMAS, P. EWOLT, S.S. WALKER, P. HENRY, 1st B DOWIE, C. WINN, P.

WITTAKER, P. NITZE, C. MARTINA, P. SCHICK, O.F. KNAUPP, 2nd B FOSS 3rd B

Larry Gilbert's 1923 pennant-winning team. (Courtesy Arthur O. Schott)

CHAPTER NINE

Take Me Out
to the Ball Game

*The Heinemann Park press box was a gathering place for local gamblers
on their day off. They would sit around making bets while listening to the
play-by-play coming in on the sports wire. They'd bet on each pitch,
whether it was a ball or a strike. They'd bet on anything.*
F. Edward Hebert, *The Last of the Titans*

BASEBALL WAS THE ONLY SPORT to have a professional team, albeit a minor league team, in New Orleans in the twenties. That team was the Pelicans. As the decade opened, Johnny Dobbs, who had enjoyed a major league career with Cincinnati, Chicago, and Brooklyn, was manager. During his time with the Pelicans, 1914-22, his team did not finish lower than third.

Dobbs was known for an acid tongue, which he used on his own players as well as his opponents. He shouted throughout the game, and afterwards, had the team doctor spray his throat. He left New Orleans for Memphis in 1922.

LARRY GILBERT, MR. BASEBALL OF NEW ORLEANS

During Dobbs' stay, one of the stars of his club was a young man by the name of Larry Gilbert, who was soon to be given a title that he held without dispute, "Mr. Baseball of New Orleans."

Even as a young boy, Gilbert was involved with the Pelicans. As a youth, he was a scoreboard keeper. Later the Pels occasionally let him pitch baseball practice. His first professional contract was with Boston, where he was a member of the "1914 Miracle Braves." He was the first New Orleanian ever to play in the major leagues and the first to play in the World Series. In 1916, he was sold to Kansas City, but New Orleans stepped in and offered Kansas City $2,500 for him, a record price at the time. It was accepted and he became a Pelican.

After Dobbs' exit in 1922, Gilbert was named manager of the team and led the Pels to an unequaled reign over the Southern Association. With a break of only one year—1932, when Jake Atz took over and Gilbert moved into the front office—Gilbert was manager from 1923 to 1938. During these years he won five pennants (1923, 1926, 1927, 1933, and 1934). His teams finished out of the first division only once, in 1931.

MEL OTT, ONE OF NEW ORLEANS' GREATEST

Melvin Thomas Ott, from Gretna on the West Bank of New Orleans, was probably the greatest baseball player to come out of the New Orleans area. His

Larry Gilbert, Mr. Baseball of New Orleans, was the first New Orleanian ever to play in the major leagues (Boston Braves) and the first to play in a World Series. He was named manager of the Pelicans in 1922 and, with a break of only one year (1932), managed the team from 1923 to 1938. During these years, his team won five pennants in the Southern Association. (Courtesy Arthur O. Schott)

115

twenty-two-year career with the New York Giants began in 1926. During his career, he hit 511 home runs to set a National League record. He retired with a lifetime batting average of .304.

"HEINE" AND HIS OLD STRAW HAT

One of the most controversial men ever to come upon the sports scene in New Orleans was Alexander Julius Heinemann, nicknamed "Heine." A soft-drink peddler in the old Pelican Stadium, he was an officer in the club by 1904 and its president in 1914.

The Pelicans were almost bankrupt in 1914. Their ball park was at Carrollton and Banks, where the Jesuit gymnasium is today. Under Heinemann's direction, in 1914-15, the Pels moved the grandstand piece by piece to Carrollton and Tulane, and began to win games and make money. It was Heine who brought in Johnny Dobbs and later arranged for the purchase of Larry Gilbert.

There was probably never a pair of baseball executives who worked in such close harmony as Heine and Larry Gilbert. Under their combined leadership, the Pels enjoyed their glory days, as Larry brought five pennants to the city.

Heine was not a great favorite with the New Orleans spectators. On special occasions, he'd change from his alpaca coat to an outfit that included a stiff collar, a fancy cravat, and a dusty old stiff straw hat. Then he'd roam the stands, peering up at the skies for a sign of rain, and the crowds would cry "Cheapskate" and "Skinflint." He did it, he said, "because the crowds seemed to like it and they paid good money to get in."

By the twenties, he'd developed the franchise into "one of the most valuable pieces of minor league property in the United States," according to a local newspaper.

He dabbled in the stock market, and in the crash of 1929 he was badly hit. He had advised others to buy stocks and felt guilty over their losses. In 1930, Heine took his own life.

Alexander Julius Heinemann, nicknamed "Heine" (1876-1930), was largely responsible for the development of the Pelican baseball team into one of the most valuable minor league properties in the country. Starting as a soft-drink vendor in Pelican Park, he became manager. He had the stadium moved from Carrollton and Banks to Carrollton and Tulane. It was then called Heinemann Park. He ended his own life in 1930. (Courtesy Arthur O. Schott)

A PART OF OUR LIVES

"Baseball was a part of our lives," says baseball historian Arthur Schott. "There was no television yet and no air-conditioning. If you walked along the sidewalks, the windows were all open, and from each window you could hear the radio broadcasting the baseball game being recreated in the studio by Jack Halliday off the ticker tape. In later years, you could hear Ted Andrews doing the game live from the stadium."

The ball park was called Heinemann Park from 1915 to 1938. Then the name was changed to Pelican Stadium, and so it was called until 1957 when the Pels departed the ball park at Tulane and South Carrollton Avenue.

In the twenties, baseball was always played in the daytime. It was not until August 5, 1930 that the Pels played baseball under the lights.

THE GOLDEN AGE OF BOXING IN NEW ORLEANS

New Orleans was a boxing mecca in the late nineteenth and early twentieth centuries. In the Coliseum Arena in New Orleans in 1924, Gene Tunney defeated local boxer Marty Burke.

"Shoeless" Joe Jackson played in the Carolinas in his bare feet, complaining that the rough field made the ball "wingy." Here he seems to be doing all right in shoes. He played for the Pelicans and later for the Chicago White Sox. (Courtesy Lloyd W. Huber for the late Leonard V. Huber)

Pete Herman, born in New Orleans, won the world bantam-weight title from Kid Williams in 1917, lost it to Joe Lynch in 1920, and regained it from Lynch in 1921. He was selected for the Hall of Fame. (Courtesy Lloyd W. Huber for the late Leonard V. Huber)

Tony Canzoneri, born in Slidell, rose from a shoeshine boy around New Orleans to one of the greatest lightweights of all time. During his career, he held eight titles, including his amateur championships. He was selected for the Boxing Hall of Fame. (Courtesy Lloyd W. Huber for the late Leonard V. Huber)

Harry Wills, a powerful heavyweight born in New Orleans in 1889, fought for over twenty years. (Courtesy Lloyd W. Huber for the late Leonard V. Huber)

Pal Moran fought seven world champions. He fought Jack Bernstein in 1923, and Rocky Kansas and Kid Kaplan in 1926. (Courtesy Lloyd W. Huber for the late Leonard V. Huber)

New Orleans produced scores of boxers, many of whom never quite reached the top. But two made the Hall of Fame: Tony Canzoneri and Pete Herman. Canzoneri, born in Slidell, Louisiana, once a shoeshine boy in New Orleans, became one of the greatest lightweight boxers of all time. He started as an amateur at 5'4", weighing only ninety-five pounds. During his career, he held eight titles in the 1920s and the 1930s.

Pete Herman, born Peter Gulotta of Italian parents, started his boxing career in 1912. He won the world bantamweight title from Kid Williams in New Orleans in 1917. He lost it to Joe Lynch in 1917 in Madison Square Gardens in New York, but went on to do what few fighters ever do. He regained his title on July 25, 1921, when he beat Joe Lynch in Brooklyn in fifteen rounds, only to lose it two months later to Johnny Buff. Pete Herman fought his last fight in April 1922, when he beat Roy Moore in a ten-rounder in Boston. Failing eyesight forced him to retire.

Three other fighters born in New Orleans have been rated as nationally important by Nat Fleischer, publisher of *Ring* magazine. Harry Wills, a powerful heavyweight, fought for over twenty years, ending in 1932, when he was knocked out in Brooklyn by Jankassa. Pal Moran, who grew up in the French Market neighborhood, fought seven world champions between 1912 and 1929. He fought Rocky Kansas in 1926, featherweight champion Kid Kaplan the same year, and junior lightweight champion Jack Bernstein in 1923. The third Fleischer selection was Joe ("Baker Boy") Mandot, one of the most popular boxers of the Crescent City.

Joe Mandot, the "baker boy" who was the pride of the French Market area, fought eight men who became world champions, losing decisively to only one. He fought Ad Wolgast, Willie Ritchie, Freddie Welsh, and others. (Courtesy Lloyd W. Huber for the late Leonard V. Huber)

BOXING EXHIBITIONS AT THE HOLLAND HOUSE

Pictures of Pete Herman, Joe Mandot, and other boxers hung on the walls at the Holland House (today's Tavern on the Park). Many still called it Lamothe's Restaurant, since it had been managed by Frank Lamothe for a decade before 1922, when ownership passed to Anthony Campagno and his sons Nick and Dominic. It was Lamothe who had left the restaurant with a legacy of sports figures and jazz musicians.

Throughout the twenties, boxing exhibition matches were held on Friday nights at the Holland House (Lamothe's). A ring was squared off and outstanding prizefighters like Joe Mandot fought there, drawing spectators in great numbers. Beansy Fauria ran a bookie parlor in the back, and many of the heavy gamblers bet there, because of its proximity to the Fair Grounds Race Track. Prohibition never bothered the drinkers at the Holland House, where first-rate scotch and rye was served. (See "Prohibition," chapter 10.)

FOOTBALL

In 1915, Clark D. Shaughnessy came to Tulane University as football coach, and with the exception of 1921, coached the Green Wave team for ten years. Under his guidance, Tulane became a major competitor in Southern collegiate football. His greatest teams were those of 1924, which upset Vanderbilt, and 1925, which went unbeaten.

In the years 1920 to 1940, Tulane enjoyed its golden age of football. Two coaches directed the team in the twenties: Clark Shaughnessy, 1915-20, 1922-

Grand Stand at
Fair Grounds Race Track,
New Orleans, La.—105

*The Fair Grounds Race Track, owned by the Business Men's Racing Association, seated 5,000.
The annual season extended from January 1 to Mardi Gras. In 1924, 1,130 horses participated.*

*The Tulane football team of 1925, captained by Lester J. Lautenschlaeger, won all their games
except for a tie with Missouri. Clark Shaughnessy was their coach. Charles ("Peggy") Flournoy
was named All-American. (Courtesy Lloyd W. Huber for the late Leonard V. Huber)*

26; and Bernie Bierman, 1927-31. During that time, two Greenies were named All-American players: Charles ("Peggy") Flournoy, 1925; and Willis ("Bill") Banker, 1929.

Bernie Bierman was taken on as an assistant coach by Shaughnessy in 1923. He left three years later to become head coach at Mississippi A&M (now Mississippi State). When Shaughnessy left Tulane for Loyola in 1927, Bierman returned to Tulane. His 1929, 1930, and 1931 teams were unbeaten in the South, and he took the '31 team to the Rose Bowl.

There was no Sugar Bowl game in New Orleans in the twenties; the first Sugar Bowl game was played in 1935.

Coach Bernie Bierman became head coach at Tulane in 1927. His '29, '30, and '31 teams were unbeaten in the South. (Courtesy Lloyd W. Huber for the late Leonard V. Huber)

THE FIGHTING TIGERS OF LSU

In 1920, the new head football coach at LSU (Tulane's arch rival) was Branch Bocock. Although the 1920 and 1921 seasons had winning records, LSU did not beat Tulane, and that was all that mattered. Bocock was asked to resign.

Clarence ("Fatty") Ives, a spectacular punter, and Newton ("Dirty") Helm, a running back, were the outstanding players in those years. The football was inflated by mouth in those days, and the valve tucked under a piece of leather. By kicking *away* from the valve, Ives gave more momentum to his spiral kicks. "They were so high," said Tad Gormley, track and assistant football coach, "that the safety man could have gone over and sat on a chair waiting for it to come down." Ives was voted best athlete at LSU in 1919 and 1920. He was one of the three four-letter men in LSU history.

When Bocock left, Irving Pray, who had coached the Tigers in 1919, returned. In the second game of 1922, Loyola came up from New Orleans and defeated the Tigers 7-0. When LSU met Tulane, it was with a 2-7 record. But the Tigers defeated the Green Wave 25-14, and the memory of the season's heavy losses was obliterated in one afternooon.

The day after this upset, however, LSU officials offered Mike Donahue, coach at Auburn, a five-year contract at $10,000 a year. Donahue took the job.

On Thanksgiving Day in 1923, Tulane defeated the Tigers with a score of 13-0. The Green Wave couldn't miss, with a 7-1 record and players like Lester Lautenschlaeger, "Brother" Brown, and "Peggy" Flournoy. The game, the first broadcast over radio, presaged an era of big-time football in southern Louisiana.

In 1925 LSU defeated Loyola 13-0, but lost to a powerful Tulane team, 16-0. Coach Donahue was replaced in 1927 by thirty-two-year-old Russ Cohen from Alabama. Tulane also changed coaches—Bernie Bierman for Clark Shaughnessy.

On November 28, 1928, Governor Huey P. Long, sitting in his Tiger Stadium box, witnessed the defeat of LSU 21-0. Long told everyone within hearing distance, "Banker is too good a player to be at Tulane. He'll be playing for LSU next season." He wouldn't, of course. There were such things as transfer rules, but Long couldn't be bothered with tiresome details.

Some of LSU's great players of the twenties were "Babe" Godfrey, "Hinky" Haynes, Martin Flood, Jess Tinsley, and Guy Nesom. The Tigers' Jess Tinsley and Tulane's Bill Banker were selected in 1928 to the All-Southern team.

LOYOLA, A GRIDIRON POWER

Loyola University yearbooks of the twenties show that the football coaches were Richard Ducote, Eddie Reed, and Nat Tyler. The team captain was Gene Walet, who played end. Other outstanding players were Louis ("Red") Gremillion, running back; Harold Winling; Anthony Schiro; and J. R. ("Deuce") Domengeaux.

Under the direction of Eddie Reed, in his first and only year of varsity coaching, the Loyola University football team of 1926 played to a final record of 10-0, defeating such powerful opponents as Baylor, Detroit, and Catholic University of Washington, D.C. The "Maroon Cyclone" captured the national scoring title of 355 points while allowing only 30. The squad's most outstanding player was Elton ("Bucky") Moore, running back, dubbed "The Dixie Flyer" by the Newspaper Enterprise Association.

Loyola's Wolfpack of 1926 had the best record of all major universities in the country. They were undefeated and untied. In the back row, third from left, was Elton ("Bucky") Moore, a running back called "The Dixie Flyer" who was the star of the team. In the second row, far right, is F. Edward Hebert, director of publicity, later a U.S. congressman. In the second row, left, were Coach James Edward Reed and Manager Louis Maumas. (Courtesy Loyola University)

Wearing a helmet was optional in 1926. Helmets were little protection in any case with their thin cotton padding. The skimpy uniforms didn't provide much protection, either. And football cleats were usually attached to a pair of old shoes.

In 1927, Coach Reed was replaced by Clark Shaughnessy, who came over from Tulane. An interesting game was the one played against the Haskell Indians, who paraded at half time in full feathered headdress, with their ponies. Haskell Institute is now Kansas State.

The 1928 team, coached by Shaughnessy, had a season record of 7-3. Notre Dame beat Loyola that year with a score of 12-6. The score was tied 6-6 until the last minute of play, when Knute Rockne managed to direct Neimic into scoring position. After three attempts, Neimic crossed the goal line. After this game, Rockne selected Loyola's Pete Miller for his All-American team.

Outstanding players were Raymond ("Tiny") Drouilhet, tackle; Ambrose ("Ham") Weddle, fullback; Charlie Jaubert, center; Clem Sehrt, tackle; "Zeke" Bonura, tackle; and "Bucky" Moore, halfback.

LOCAL VARSITY STADIUMS

In 1923, on Thanksgiving Day, LSU played in its new stadium for the first time, hosting Tulane. Tulane won 13-0.

Loyola's football field, with bleachers left and right and gymnasium to the rear (white building) on Freret Street, is the place where the "Maroon Cyclone" blew under Coach Eddie Reed. (Courtesy Loyola University)

Tulane Stadium, built in 1926, was not only the home of the Green Wave and the arena where every major sports event in New Orleans would take place for decades, but would also be the home of the Sugar Bowl from 1937 until the Superdome opened in 1975. The stadium, in Uptown New Orleans on Willow Street, could in time seat 81,000 spectators. It was razed in 1979.

Loyola's football stadium went up in 1928 on the Loyola campus between Bobet Hall and the gymnasium on Freret Street.

A TASTE OF PRO FOOTBALL IN NEW ORLEANS

Pro football was seen briefly in New Orleans in the mid-twenties, according to F. Edward Hebert, who was then doing public relations for Loyola. It was in its early stages, and its main attraction was Harold ("Red") Grange, the "Galloping Ghost." A big-time promotor, C. C. ("Cash & Carry") Pyle, had signed Grange to a contract and took the Chicago Bears on the road, playing select teams across the country.

In New Orleans, the Bears were to play the Southern All-Stars, a group of former college players. Grange was, of course, the main attraction. In the line was George Halas, who eventually owned the team and is called the father of professional football. In his pregame hype, Hebert promised that the fans would

125

see "the greatest collection of football celebrities ever assembled on a local grid-iron."

The lineup from Dixie included five former Tulane stars: "Brother" Brown, Bill Besselman, Gene Bergeret, Johnny Wight, and Lester Lautenschlaeger, who was later in the Football Hall of Fame. Despite losing 14-0, the Southerners played a great game, holding Grange to one touchdown.

BASKETBALL, TRACK, AND BASEBALL AT LOYOLA

In 1927, Barry Barrodale was managing the basketball team at Loyola. In 1932, he would be manager of the Olympic Boxing Team. "He was a man who could do anything," said Al Kreider, football and baseball player at Jesuit and Loyola in the twenties.

On the basketball team of 1927, "Zeke" Bonura, later of baseball major league fame, played center; Emmett Toppino (also a track sprinter) and Dave Kiefer played forward. In 1928, Noland Richards and "Bum" Heir, new additions, played forward.

Trainer Tad Gormley, for whom the City Park Stadium was named, was at LSU first, then came to Loyola.

The 1927 baseball team had several fine players: Al ("Goat") Kreider, third base; Herbie Pourciau, outfielder; Charlie Mitchell, catcher; Louis LeBlanc, first baseman; and Barry Barrodale, pitcher. In 1928, an addition was "Brute" Galle, pitcher.

Teams regularly on Loyola's schedule were Spring Hill, Southwestern in Lafayette, and Jefferson College (today's Manresa Retreat House).

PREP FOOTBALL IN NEW ORLEANS

At the outset of the twenties, there was only one public boys' high school in the city, called, appropriately enough, Boys' High (later Warren Easton), at 3019 Canal. There were only two public girls' high schools: Girls' High (later John McDonogh), at 2426 Esplanade (for the downtown girls); and Sophie B. Wright, at 1426 Napoleon Avenue (for the uptown girls). Later in the twenties, there was Alcee Fortier High School for boys, at 5624 Freret Street, and Samuel J. Peters (a commercial high school called "Commy" High) for boys, at 425 South Broad.

These three public boys' high schools—Easton, Fortier, and Peters—were the only public schools in the prep league at the end of the twenties. The Catholic boys' high schools in the league were Jesuit High, which had moved from Baronne and Gravier in 1910 to Carrollton and Palmyra; St. Aloysius High, on the corner of Esplanade and Rampart; and Holy Cross High, at 4950 Dauphine. These six schools (three public, three Catholic) comprised the Prep Football League of New Orleans.

From the beginning, Jesuit and Easton had the same kind of "grudge rivalry" that excited spectators as Tulane and LSU did. It was always a hard-fought game. Usually, Jesuit had the best Catholic school team and Easton the best public school team in the league.

Jesuit, in 1925, was coached by Bill Healy. Its most outstanding player was Elton ("Bucky") Moore, who went on to football fame at Loyola. Another was Emmett Toppino, who was a running back in football and also played basketball, baseball, and ran track. "Shorty" Gannon was an outstanding halfback of the twenties. Tom Daigle was a running back, and his brother Eddie was a football

The 1927-28 Loyola University frosh basketball team included Emmett Toppino and Zeke Bonura, the school's all-time Hall-of-Famers. As a sprinter in the '32 Los Angeles Olympics, Toppino was a member of the 400-meter relay team. Bonura played baseball for the Chicago White Sox from 1934 to 1937 and held the javelin record for many decades beginning in the twenties. (Courtesy Rev. Thomas Clancy and Loyola University)

The Jesuit High School football team. Top row: F. Courrages, John Watermeier, Country Gilmore, John Manning, Jake Kreiger, Sonny Winters. Second row: Max Gougeot, manager, Clem Sehrt, Weilbacher, J. Madden, Fr. Martin, Coach Bill Healey, Ray Mock, Bob Landry, Doc Erskine. Third row: Joseph Vella, Ike Favalora, Leo Blessing, Bob Morris, Clarence Hebert, Mike White, Shorty Gannon, William Snee. Fourth row: W. Aitkens, Emmett Toppino, John De Buys, Man Montagnet, captain, Joseph Fazzio, Sid Danjean. Most players did not wear helmets, as it was not compulsory. (Courtesy Dr. Bob Morris)

star at Aloysius. Others worthy of mention at Jesuit were Pete Miller, lineman; "Lizzy" Ford; and Al Kreider, guard, who later played football and baseball for Loyola from 1926 to 1929.

Holy Cross always had a good team and was always a contender, sometimes winning the Prep League play-offs. An outstanding player for Fortier High School in the twenties was Jack Pazzana.

The Anheuser-Busch Brewery at Gravier and South Front streets stayed in business during Prohibition by ingeniously diversifying, as can be seen by the ICE CREAM sign on the side of the trucks. When New Orleans went back to drinking beer, the company moved to larger quarters. (Courtesy Anthony T. Mandina)

CHAPTER TEN

Prohibition: The Great National Drought

Mother makes brandy from cherries; Pop distills whiskey and gin; Sister sells
wine from the grapes on our vine— Good grief, how the money rolls in!
Anonymous, printed in the New York *World*

"UNCLE SAM DOESN'T ALLOW LIQUOR at Annapolis," said William Jennings Bryan, speaking to a crowd of 2,000 New Orleanians at the Athenaeum Theater Sunday, January 28, 1917. "If he is so interested in his wards [that] he will not permit them to drink, why do New Orleans parents allow their boys to patronize saloons? If Uncle Sam's young men go wrong, he can get others. But when your boys go down into the pit of misery, can you get them?" (or, can you get "others?" This was not exactly a logical or literary analogy, but Bryan was known better for his fist-pounding, fire-and-brimstone orations than for making sense.)

The former secretary of state was speaking against the consumption of alcohol, as the United States moved closer and closer to national Prohibition.

PROHIBITION DIDN'T HAVE A PRAYER
IN NEW ORLEANS

Just as surely as the Volstead Act was passed in 1919, and the enforcement of Prohibition was attempted in the Crescent City in the twenties, Orleanians found a way to get around the law. Natives of the "City that Care Forgot" were not about to stop drowning their sorrows in gin, even if it had to be bathtub gin.

"There was no way to stop people from sellin' liquor in this town," said Harry Gregson, police captain in charge of the Basin Street area in the twenties (when interviewed in 1966). "Most of what they *did* sell was poison. If you wanted the real thing, you went to Tom Anderson's on Rampart Street or to Lamothe's out at the park."

On June 30, 1919, the eve of "the Great Experiment," in the *Times-Picayune*, Mayor Martin Behrman announced that the Police Department would make every effort to enforce the law and to assist federal government authorities in its enforcement. Citizens wondered how they would accomplish this, since neither the Department of Justice nor the Internal Revenue Department had increased their staff.

PRESIDENT WILSON STATES HIS VIEWS

President Woodrow Wilson stated a day earlier that as soon as demobilization of troops (from World War I) was complete, he might lift the prohibition of liquor. Prohibition had been a wartime measure passed to keep servicemen on the alert and out of trouble. Wilson's announcement encouraged New Orleans saloon owners to keep their stock until January 1, 1920, when they might be permitted to reopen.

The policy to be adopted the first dry day, July 1, 1919, was that most saloons were to be closed or were to open as restaurants or soda fountains. Some stated that they would continue to sell beer containing not more than 2.75 percent alcohol. The Internal Revenue Department ruling was that anything beyond one-half of 1 percent alcohol was intoxicating. The percentage of alcohol in beer was one of the big discrepancies to be resolved. The newspapers said that authorities would probably move against the sale of beverages having more than 2.75 percent alcohol first. The penalty for violation was set at $1,000 fine or imprisonment or both.

Saloonmen asked the Internal Revenue Department all day June 29, 1919, what they should do with their stock—leave it in their saloons or store it at home? Since no rulings were made on this, each saloonkeeper was on his own.

Headlines in the *Times-Picayune* of June 30, 1919, read:

VISITORS FROM DRY STATES RUSH HERE
SALOONS CLOSE AT MIDNIGHT

> A few formal celebrations will take place at cafes, clubs, and hotels, and large crowds are expected at each. All New Orleanians and visitors from dry territories in Louisiana, Mississippi, Alabama, Arkansas, and Texas are preparing for the farewell to "Mr. John Barleycorn," and Supt. of Police Pat Mooney is expecting "a hot time in the old town tonight." At least 25 extra policemen plus the regular force in downtown will be needed to suppress the hilarity.

On July 1, 1919, the *Times-Picayune* announced:

> Attorney General Palmer, pending court decision, will not prosecute sales of beverages containing 2.75% alcohol or less. The right to buy and sell liquor was prohibited at midnight, June 30, 1919. It will not become legal until the demobilization of the army, and on January 16, 1920, it will be prohibited by constitutional amendment.

WHISKEY AS MEDICINE?

On July 9, 1919, Congressman Caldwell reminded the House of Representatives that in the 1918 influenza epidemic, whiskey was the standard remedy. Congressman Layton of Delaware said that was not true. Congressman Small of North Carolina attacked the bill on grounds that it was unconstitutional to pass legislature for the enforcement of a war measure when the war was over.

On January 22, 1920, the *Times-Picayune* reported that Chief of Internal Revenue Rufus W. Fontenot "is earnestly requesting druggists to exercise discretion in the dispensing of whiskey as a medical remedy, and they will be lending the department valuable assistance." They were not to "sell bay rum or any other preparation containing an excess of the legal amount of alcohol unless they were convinced the customer does not intend to drink it as a beverage."

Headlines of the New Orleans *States* on January 1, 1920 read: *OLD MAN BARLEYCORN BURIED IN FLOOD OF LIQUOR; NEW YEAR GREETED BY BIG CROWDS IN RESTAURANTS AND STREETS.* In the churches, night services were held and thanks were given for a dry America in 1920. In the restaurants, "Happy New Year" was shouted out, echoed by jazz bands and screamed by hundreds of steam whistles on craft on the river.

It was perhaps the last welcome New Orleans would give the New Year with wine and other intoxicating liquors, and everyone who had a quart or a pint of whiskey, gin, wine, champagne, or liqueur lifted his glass to the coming year. Crowds came to Canal Street, and at midnight, there was a display of fireworks. Factory whistles, church bells, and chimes rang out.

On July 10, 1921, the newspaper announced:

RAIDED BREWERIES AGREE TO PAY U.S. $100,000 IN FINES

Prohibition officials have "drawn first blood" in their effort to establish the legality of a recent action . . . in raiding and closing six New Orleans breweries. The brewing companies will pay the government in excess of $100,000. The brewery officials are still liable to prosecution for violation of the Volstead Act.

On March 20, 1926, the New Orleans *Item* announced, "LIQUOR SQUAD RAIDS ANNUAL CAR-MEN BALL; ELEVEN JAILED, HELD IN CELLS ALL NIGHT." And on November 21, 1926: "ABSINTHE HOUSE CLOSED BY INJUNCTION OF U.S. COURT. The doors of the historic Old Absinthe House were closed on its hundredth anniversary Saturday when the U.S. Marshal nailed them together following a padlock injunction." But the revelry went on, and neither law nor injunctions could stop New Orleanians from imbibing.

TOM ANDERSON'S SALOON

Even after the closing of Storyville (1917), that infamous "red-light district" whose most beautiful and elaborate "houses" faced Basin Street, Tom Anderson's Saloon at Basin and Iberville remained in business and served hard liquor. By 1922, Tom Anderson's "restaurant" had moved to Rampart Street.

Anderson's wife had been a madam at the "fancy" house next door to the saloon on Basin Street, and after she closed her business, she and Mr. Anderson (by her own admission in an interview in the sixties) often took outings to Old Spanish Fort or to Lamothe's Tavern where Anderson had a bourbon or two, and she ordered lithia water. Then they'd dance. There was always a good band at Lamothe's.

LAMOTHE'S TAVERN

Lamothe's Tavern (today's Tavern on the Park), built in a pie-slice of land between Dumaine Street and City Park Avenue, had been, at the turn of the century, a gourmet restaurant. In 1912, at a sheriff's sale, ownership had passed to the New Orleans Brewing Company, brewers of Double Eagle—4xxxx beer, a company that was seeking outlets for its product. The brewing company leased it to Frank Lamothe from 1912 to 1919, and it became known as Lamothe's City Park Restaurant. They advertised "fine banquet hall and accommodations for ladies."

Frank Lamothe managed to combine an elite clientele with the "ladies" from Storyville. This was where the "ladies" relaxed in their free time, sitting on the upstairs balcony overlooking the entrance to City Park, watching cars and horse-drawn vehicles go in and out of the entranceway, while enjoying a cocktail and a good steak.

A cook at the tavern made the best crawfish étouffé in town, and some people went there just for that.

With the closing of Storyville, the prominent days of the restaurant ended, and by 1922, so did Frank Lamothe's management there. But he left a legacy of sports figures and early ragtime and jazz musicians. Pete Herman and his brother, Gaspar Gulotta, frequented the tavern in the twenties. Gulotta was a Bourbon Street cafe owner. Gulotta and his friends spent most of their time in the French Quarter clubs, but Pete Herman sometimes went out to the Holland House with other fighters. Lamothe had hung all their pictures on the walls: fighters, ball players, jockeys.

Boxers Pete Herman, Joe ("Baker Boy") Mandot, and Joe Rivers continued to frequent the restaurant, as well as musicians like Ben Harney, composer of the first published ragtime song, "Mr. Johnson, Turn Me Loose." Harney performed there, along with bandleaders Dominic Barroco, Charlie Fishbein, Max Fink, Emile Tosso, Lucien Broekhoeven, Giuseppe Alessandra, Siegfried Christensen, and Armand Veazey, who had led the band at the opening of the City Park racetrack back in 1905.

After Prohibition came in 1919, the New Orleans Brewing Company tried to keep its head above water by bottling root beer, but they sold the restaurant in 1922 to the Campagnos, Anthony and his sons Nick and Dominic, who operated it as the Holland House.

THE HOLLAND HOUSE IN THE ROARING TWENTIES

It was the Roaring Twenties, and the Holland House was one of the "in" places to go. The Campagnos operated an elegant restaurant on the upper floor, an ice-cream parlor on the ground floor, and a barroom to the rear. The bar was known for "the best Manhattan cocktails in town," made by Nick Campagno.

The Holland House was not the only place liquor was served in New Orleans during Prohibition. The Southern Yacht Club, a meeting place for the elite of the city, held dances twice a week at which a jazz band played, and where their own famous drink was served, the Pink Lady, also called the Pink Shimmy. The recipe called for one egg white, one teaspoon grenadine, one teaspoon sweet cream, and 1½ ounces gin. It was then shaken with ice and strained into a cocktail glass.

GAMBLING AT THE HOLLAND HOUSE

The Campagnos also rented out a back room at the Holland House to Robert ("Beansy") Fauria, who ran a bookie parlor. During the twenties and thirties, Beansy was New Orleans' best-known gambler. The Campagnos allowed him to carry on his gambling operation on their property in exchange for his help in getting first-rate scotch and rye from Honduras, liquor that had been made in England and Canada. Beansy had a police captain as a bodyguard and was never bothered by raids.

Since the tavern was near the racetrack, and many of the big gamblers came there, it was convenient all around to have a bookie on the premises.

We know from newspaper articles and stories written in the twenties that there were, during Prohibition, many speakeasies in the French Quarter, sometimes as many as three to a block, and none too well concealed. One was the old Press Club, which was a nice place to go. The others were mostly dirty and often scenes of violence—even murder.

This no doubt went hand in hand with the movement into the Quarter of the "ladies" of Storyville, which had been shut down in 1917. These prostitutes, seeking employment elsewhere, found it in the adjacent neighborhood, the French Quarter. Along Bienville, Conti, Dauphine, and St. Louis streets were lines of houses of prostitution, many nothing more than filthy cribs, replacing what had been the most elegant red-light district in the nation, on Basin Street. Now the ladies of the evening were rubbing elbows with the Creoles of the city. In time, others of their sordid ilk from distant cities would join them in the Quarter in the twenties.

VICE IN THE VIEUX CARRE IN THE TWENTIES

Vice was rampant in the Vieux Carré. Women stood in their doorways, behind slatted blinds, or in windows, naked or almost naked, calling out to men as they passed by. Competition was keen and labor was cheap. Some even seized men as they went by and tried to talk them into "doing business."

The twenties witnessed the birth of Bourbon Street as a street of sin. Saloons proliferated, ugly and dirty, some featuring stripteasers as "exotic" dancers. These were the women who invented "bumps and grinds," embellishing their acts with hand movements as come-ons to men passing by in the street. Their duties included enticing men to buy drinks at exorbitant prices.

The French Quarter held the worst dens of iniquity in the city. Other drinking places, like the Holland House, in the suburbs, were on a higher plane. Any saloon or restaurant where liquor was served became an illegitimate business, subject to seizure, and therefore a place where other illegal activities like gambling and prostitution might also be likely to thrive.

NIGHT SPOTS IN JEFFERSON PARISH

In night spots and gambling casinos in Jefferson Parish like the Suburban Gardens Club and Club Forest, liquor flowed, dice rolled, and music played on. Club Forest featured top entertainers, like Ella Logan, who went on to become famous on Broadway, and singer Tony Martin, who played a saxophone there. Other entertainers in "the Parish" included Louis Armstrong, Vincent Lopez, Fred Waring and his Pennsylvanians, Ted Weems, and Jan Garber.

THE LAW, IT SEEMS, ONLY MADE THINGS WORSE

More arrests were made for drunkenness during Prohibition than before. There was only so much the police could do when trying to enforce Prohibition in a city like New Orleans. The law created dens of sin and vice where there had been none, just so that liquor, now forbidden, could be obtained. And so it continued until 1933, when Prohibition was repealed.

"DO IT YOURSELF" BOOZE

People who were unaccustomed to frequenting nightclubs, and did not care to consort with the common element found in speakeasies, but who liked an occasional drink, made their booze at home. My husband tells a story about his grandfather who made "home brew" on one occasion. Anyone could buy the necessary ingredients: prunes, apples, bananas, watermelons, potato peelings, oats or barley. For six or seven dollars, a portable still could be purchased in any hardware store. And in the public library, it was easy enough to find books, magazines, even government pamphlets explaining the process of distillation.

It was a simple matter to get ingredients that, when mixed together, would turn to alcohol. The vintners of California sold a legal product called Vine-Glo, a grape juice that, when put in the cellar and nursed for sixty days, would turn into wine that was 15 percent alcohol.

As for beer, some brewer came up with the idea of halting the process of beer making before there was any alcohol in it at all, and selling the legal half-brewed product, called wort, along with a package of yeast that would bring it the rest of the way. This was the route my husband's grandfather followed. It took quite a while to master the art, but finally one weekend, with the help of his sons, Grampaw filled dozens of bottles of beer, corked them, and put them under the house to "age."

Exhausted from his efforts, he went to bed. In the middle of the night, a crack rang out like a gunshot, followed by another and another. It was the Fourth of July beneath Grampaw's house. All the bottles were popping their corks, and many days' effort and a lot of good home brew went down the drain.

Multiply this "cottage industry" ten-thousandfold and you might come close to the activity that was going on all over the country to bypass the Volstead Act.

CHAPTER ELEVEN

Art and Architecture

Fine art and industrial art came together, and Art Deco was born.

IN 1921, THE VIEUX CARRE COMMISSION was established, and by state amendment in 1936, was given the power to regulate architecture in the Quarter through control of building permits. Its purpose was to renovate, restore, and remodel the old buildings. The need for such an authority had become clear in the first two decades of the century, when an entire block of interesting old buildings in the Vieux Carré was demolished to build a Civil Courts Building.

Many historic buildings, still standing in the twenties, would be lost in the thirties, when the WPA moved in with federal money and labor to recondition parts of the Quarter. Slum areas would be eliminated, but "progress" as envisioned in Washington, D.C. had a different definition than it did in the minds of New Orleans preservationists. The Old Red Store (1830) would be demolished. Gallatin Street, that two-block "street of missing men," would be wiped out altogether to relieve the city of a slum area. Some would say the changes were for the better. Gallatin Street was replaced with airy steel sheds for the farmers' market, but a part of our history was gone.

COMMERCIAL ARCHITECTURE IN THE CENTRAL BUSINESS DISTRICT

After the Reconstruction Era, there was an acceleration of growth in the CBD from 1890 till the Crash of 1929. The architects at the turn of the century whose works are an important contribution to the CBD include Sully, Andry and Bendernagel, Samuel Stone, Wogan and Toledano, and Diboll, Owen, and Goldstein. Many of their works have already been demolished, but there remains a delightful "mix" of buildings from the early days of Faubourg St. Mary and modern skyscrapers, giving an architectural chronology to the CBD, which is its legacy to the future.

The Pere Marquette Building at 150 Baronne, one of New Orleans' early skyscrapers, designed in 1925 by architects Scott Joy and William E. Spink, is an example of Gothic forms used to decorate a modern skyscraper. The lower three stories are in light-colored tile and Gothic decoration like the base of a column.

135

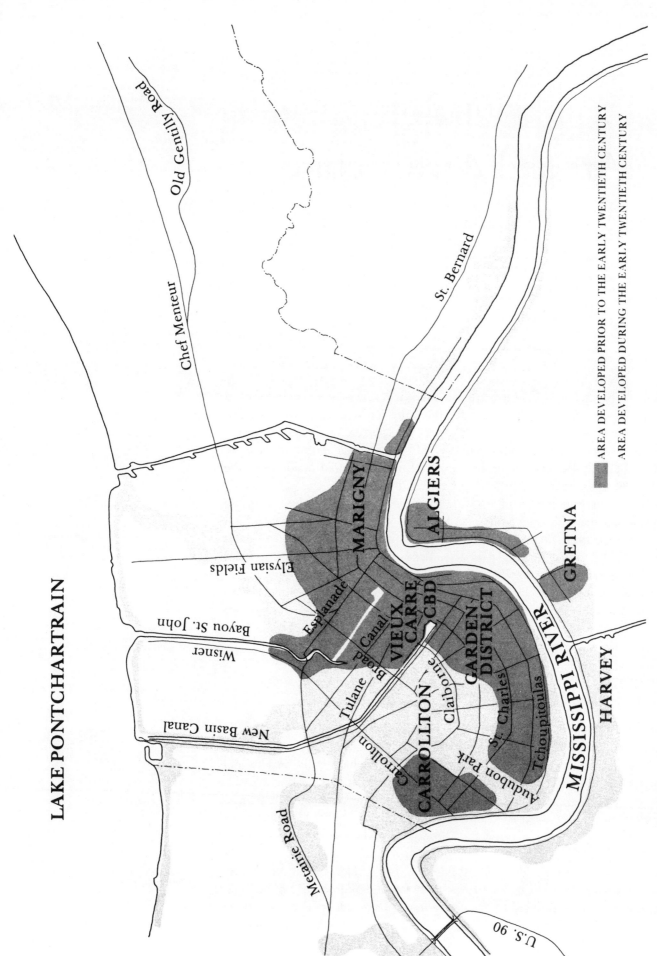

LAKE PONTCHARTRAIN

Old Gentilly Road

Chef Menteur

St. Bernard

MARIGNY

ALGIERS

Elysian Fields

GRETNA

Esplanade

VIEUX CARRE

CBD

GARDEN DISTRICT

MISSISSIPPI RIVER

Bayou St. John

Wisner

Canal

Broad

Claiborne

St. Charles

Tchoupitoulas

Tulane

Audubon Park

CARROLLTON

Carrollton

New Basin Canal

Metairie Road

HARVEY

U.S. 90

■ AREA DEVELOPED PRIOR TO THE EARLY TWENTIETH CENTURY
▓ AREA DEVELOPED DURING THE EARLY TWENTIETH CENTURY

This map shows areas developed prior to the early twentieth century, and those developed during the early twentieth century. (Courtesy Lloyd Vogt)

The next twelve stories are like the shaft of the column, and the top three are emphasized by a light stringcourse and deep pierced cornice in the capital.

The First National Bank of Commerce at 210 Baronne is the present name of a banking institution that goes back to 1831. The nineteen-story building, designed by Emile Weil and built in 1927, then housed the "Canal Bank," as it was called. It originally had three female structures at the base of the flagpole and pelican relief sculptures on the thirteenth level.

The Hibernia Bank Building on Carondelet and Gravier, designed by Favrot and Livaudais in 1921, was twenty-three stories high. The wings of the building facing Union and Gravier are fourteen stories and the tower is a landmark, officially considered a sailor's beacon. With its Indiana limestone facade, the building incorporates neo-Renaissance decoration used in the early twentieth century.

The National American Bank at 145 Carondelet was designed by architect Moise Goldstein, with Jens B. Jensen as consulting engineer. Built in 1928-29, the twenty-three-story building, faced with granite and limestone, cost $3.5 million, including the site.

An eleven-story brick building at 321 St. Charles Avenue was erected in 1920 from designs by Gen. Allison Owen for offices of the United Fruit Company. Its ornate entrance features fruit-filled cornucopia, symbolic of the banana empire. A William Woodward painting covered the oval ceiling of the entrance rotunda. The building was occupied in 1966 by the International City Bank and Trust Company.

In 1928, construction began on the current main office of the Alerion Bank at 200 Carondelet. This beautiful marble and granite structure designed by Moise Goldstein is considered a New Orleans Art Deco architectural landmark.

The Canal Bank Building on Baronne Street.

HOME CONSTRUCTION

What was new in home construction in the twenties? First of all, indoor bathrooms, which had been made possible by the new system of drainage pumps throughout the city. Secondly, indoor kitchens with porcelain sinks for hot and cold running water and gas ranges replacing wood and kerosene stoves. All these marvels made the housewife's work easier, safer, and cleaner.

The exteriors of new homes were undergoing drastic changes, showing restraint in contrast to the elaborate decorative images of turn-of-the-century Victorian homes. Architects of the twenties were designing houses in Georgian Colonial Revival and neoclassical styles. It was a time of varied tastes including such styles as beaux arts classicism, neo-Italianate, Italian Renaissance, and Dutch Colonial Revival. In contrast to the dark colors of the Victorian houses, Georgian Colonial Revival and neoclassical homes were most often painted all white. Turned wood columns were replaced by the simpler classical columns, and stained glass was losing popularity.

In New Orleans, due to a new postwar prosperity in the 1920s, construction boomed. Throughout the twenties, the city spread, as we have seen, to the north (Mid-City and Lakeview), to the south (Algiers and Gretna), and to the east (Gentilly and St. Bernard). Expansion was due in large part to the mobility provided by the automobile and the new streetcar routes.

A shotgun in the bungalow style, Carrollton Historic District. (Courtesy Donna Fricker, photographer)

Meanwhile, in the twenties, the most popular styles of moderately priced houses in New Orleans were the bungalow and the Spanish Colonial Revival. The Tudor Revival enjoyed a certain limited popularity.

The bungalow came originally from California. This style of architecture avoided machine-made ornamentation in favor of simpler elements that could be produced on the construction site. Bungalows were one- or one-and-a-half-story structures with simple lines and large projecting roofs. Construction was usually of wood frame on brick piers. The house was built of weatherboard siding, wood shingles, or stucco, and the porch was essential to the design. Porch roofs were often supported by large, square, tapered pedestals of wood, stucco, or rock, extending three feet above the porch level, with straight or tapered wooden posts on top. These posts were often paired or tripled.

The bungalow shotgun double, built in that era, is still a common sight throughout the city. This wood-framed bungalow on piers has a front gallery shaded by a gabled roof. A pair of multilight windows is often centered in the front gable. The roof is usually supported by paired, slightly tapered wooden posts. The exterior walls are of weatherboard siding.

A bungalow with an open gallery and paired columns, 1920s, Gentilly neighborhood.

A shotgun double in the bungalow style in the Carrollton Historic District. (Courtesy Donna Fricker, photographer)

A raised bungalow in the Carrollton Historic District. (Courtesy Donna Fricker, photographer)

The raised bungalow is a one-story, wood-frame house with a gallery. Wide, flared steps approach the raised landing leading to the porch, or gallery. The roof has two low-pitched gables, the front gable having a single multilight attic window. A pair of tapered columns or massive, stuccoed pedestals support the framework of the porch. Bungalows of all three varieties can be found in Old Lakeview, Gentilly, and Mid-City.

The Spanish Colonial Revival was introduced at the 1915 Panama-California Exposition in San Diego, and was modeled on the missions and houses of the Spanish in Florida and the Southwest, not on those of Spanish Colonial New Orleans. The Spanish Colonial house had a red barrel-tile roof and white stucco exterior walls, with cast-iron ornamentation around windows and doors. Many Spanish Colonial houses can be found in the Gentilly area.

The Tudor Revival house enjoyed some popularity in the years between 1910 and 1930. The distinguishing characteristics are high-pitched gabled roofs and half-timber construction with stucco infilling. The contrast between the white stucco and the dark exposed timbers is its most attractive feature. It is modeled on houses in England during the Tudor period (1485-1558).

Camelback houses were built by Orleanians who needed to add to their homes and had nowhere to build but up. Without changing the facade, they built a second story above the back part of the house, but not the front. The idea caught on, and in the years between 1870 and 1929, many camelbacks were built in the city.

The Spanish Colonial Revival house was also called "New California" style. Its features were red barrel-tile roof, white stucco exterior, and cast-iron ornamentation. These "New California" apartments were at 2127 Carondelet Street.

Camelbacks reflect the architecture of the period. A Greek Revival camelback has square posts or columns, and windows beginning at the floor. Victorian camelbacks have a great deal of gingerbread millwork on the porch or very ornate brackets. Camelbacks can be found in Mid-City or in Faubourg Treme.

STATUARY AND SCULPTURE

At City Park, near the decorative Pizatti Gate entrance on Alexander Street, was a wooden, open-air, octagon-shaped dancing platform, with jigsaw-work balusters and a pyramid roof. The "driving" bridges (as opposed to the footbridges) on Anseman Avenue and the Grandjean Bridge were all originally made of wood. They had been built in the nineteenth century for carriages, not automobiles. After the advent of the car, all bridges needed constant repair until they were replaced by cement bridges in the mid-1930s.

The most durable of the original bridges in City Park were the stone footbridges. The Langles Bridge near the Casino was built in 1902. The Pichot Bridge and the Goldfish Pond Bridge are stone spans "that go nowhere." They stand on dry land; the lagoons they once crossed have dried up.

The beaux arts scheme of urban development and sculpture was known in the world of architecture as "City Beautiful." It came from the French *Ecole des Beaux Arts* in the late nineteenth century and began to influence the development of American cities in the 1890s. In New Orleans, as early as 1900, city planners considered the "City Beautiful" concept of an entrance into City Park from the wide, elegant Esplanade that culminated at Bayou St. John. It was an accident of design, but a fortuitous one, that the avenue that followed a route from the river through several former plantations would also lead right into City Park. The plan would visually extend tree-lined Esplanade Avenue into the park along a palm-lined avenue as far as the broad, raised circle. Esplanade Avenue would become the major entrance to the park. This decision followed four major land acquisitions giving the park access to frontage on Bayou St. John.

At the outset of the twenties, the Beauregard Statue had recently been erected just outside the main entrance to the park, a steel bridge had been built over Bayou St. John at the end of Esplanade Avenue, and the Isaac Delgado Museum of Art, which stood on the broad raised circle of land at the end of the entrance avenue, had been dedicated. Lelong Avenue led from the entrance of the park to the museum. The avenue had been completed and lined with palms, and the Grandjean Bridge behind the museum had been rebuilt of steel, making the drive from Esplanade into the heart of the park easy and beautiful.

The Cotton Exchange Building, at the corner of Gravier and Carondelet, built in 1882-83, was ready for the wrecker in 1920. Five statues adorned the building, three on the third floor representing Agriculture, Industry, and Peace and two on the ground floor as column supports called caryatids. The statues were moved to City Park in the 1920s for a brief stay. The caryatids now stand in the 100 block of City Park Avenue.

A SHORT LIFE FOR NUDE STATUES
ON LELONG AVENUE

Five nude statues were placed along Lelong and Anseman avenues in 1920, but their stay was very brief. They came originally from the Cotton Exchange. Three represented Agriculture, Industry, and Peace. The other two had served as supports on a building in place of columns and were called caryatids.

The statues were disrobed and voluptuous, to the dismay of many a citizen. We can all recall a similar protest to the bare-breasted, generously endowed sculptures at the entrance to the Louisiana World's Fair Grounds in 1984. The 1984 sculptures were tolerated for the six-month tenure of the fair, but three of the 1920 statues were removed to the Metairie Cemetery and two (the caryatids) remain in the 100 block of City Park Avenue today.

ART DECO ON THE WAY

After 1925, art styles worldwide reacted to twentieth-century realities. The Paris *Exposition des Arts Decoratifs* (1925) defined a new international approach to the arts, when "the attempt to unite arts with industry embraced the machine age." Before this time, *fine* art had been the antithesis of *industrial* art. Now both came together, and Art Deco was born. Art Deco had as its basic premise the finding of strength in nature and the celebration of man and his works in highly stylized motifs. Pronounced classical statuary and architecture would soon give way to Art Deco, especially since the WPA funding of the thirties made possible the construction of so many buildings, bridges, and statues within a short period of time.

During the transitional period, a new fountain was planned for City Park, which would be called Popp Fountain. It was designed in the pronounced classical style, but by the time it was finished, it had a distinctly Art Deco centerpiece. This was due to the circumstances of its timing.

The donor, Rebecca Grant Popp, died in 1928, ten years after her husband, John F. Popp. They had both favored classic-style buildings. Mrs. Popp bequeathed $25,000 for a memorial to be erected in City Park and designed by Olmsted Brothers, traditional architects of Brookline, Massachusetts, but everything had to wait for the City Park Board to finish outlining its new master plan, which was to guide all work after that time.

Also, because its final completion required WPA aid, it was not finished until 1937. During that span of time, styles had changed. Olmsted Brothers designed the *pergola* or architectural trellis and twenty-six columns that surround it in classical style, but the work was carried out under the direction of architect Richard Koch, and a young man named Samuel Wilson (who wrote the foreword for this book in 1992) made drawings for the inscription around the wall. It was Richard Koch who got Enrique Alferez to design the central waterspout, giving it lotuslike waves and stylized dolphins. Art Deco had by that time surpassed classicism in popular appeal. The "combination" fountain was unique inasmuch as it mirrored the changing styles of statuary in the late 1920s and the 1930s.

THE DELGADO MUSEUM OF ART

New Orleans had no better locale for an elegant museum than the circle at the end of Lelong Avenue. For the architecture of the building, the museum board had chosen from seventeen proposals a plan "inspired by Greek design, sufficiently moderated to give a sub-tropical appearance." So said the city newspapers. The building also had an excellent interior plan, allowing for a skylight to illuminate the sculpture hall, which would be surrounded by galleries.

The beautiful new Isaac Delgado Museum of Art became, in the twenties, the repository of several New Orleans collections—the Hyams Barbizon and Salon paintings, the Morgan Whitney jades, and the Howard collection of Greek pottery.

The Isaac Delgado Museum of Art, 1920 (now the New Orleans Museum of Art), in City Park at the end of Lelong Avenue.

EVOLUTION OF THE ART ASSOCIATION
OF NEW ORLEANS

B. A. Wikstrom, a Norwegian who came to New Orleans in 1883, promoted an organization known as the Artists Association of New Orleans, which held exhibits annually on Camp Street until the turn of the century. In 1901, the brothers William and Ellsworth Woodward, in charge of Newcomb Art School, promoted a new group called the Arts and Exhibitions Club, which merged with the Artists Association in 1904. The resulting Art Association of New Orleans became the artistic mainstay of the Delgado Museum of Art.

In the 1920s, the French Quarter, and New Orleans in general, was swarming with talented artists and writers. Many had been born elsewhere but eventually settled in New Orleans to do their most serious and memorable work. Among the most prolific of New Orleans artists in the twenties was Alexander John Drysdale (born in Marietta, Georgia, 1870; died in New Orleans, 1934). He was a landscape painter associated with images of misty Louisiana bayous, marshes, and large moss-laden oaks in an impressionistic style uniquely his own. His "watercolor" technique employed oil paint diluted in kerosene applied to sized board with brushes and cotton balls. His two most important commissions were oil paintings on canvas for the restaurant of D. H. Holmes department store (1927) and for the administration building of Shushan Airport (1933). He was one of the most sought-after living artists in the twenties and thirties.

Robert B. Mayfield (born in Carlinville, Illinois, 1869; died in New Orleans, 1934) was an artist who also devoted much of his life to newspaper work. As an artist, he was a painter and sketcher, active from 1892 to 1932. A member of the Art Association of New Orleans, he exhibited at the Arts and Crafts Club in 1924 and the Delgado Museum of Art in 1932. As a journalist, he was the associate editor of the *Times-Picayune* from 1920 to 1933.

Charles Woodward Hutson (born in South Carolina, 1840; died in New Orleans, 1936) was a scholar, author, and teacher, as well as an artist. After retiring as a teacher of languages and the classics at universities in nearly all the Southern states, he began to paint in earnest when he was past middle age. His earliest New Orleans subjects were pastels of French Quarter buildings, but he later turned to landscapes, coastal scenes, and respresentations of historical and classical themes. In 1923 he did a series of "Fantasies" based on Bible subjects and the classics. He exhibited regularly in New Orleans until his death.

Ronald Hargrave spent several years in New Orleans, leaving his paintings in the city. He did portraits and a series of colored etchings that hung in the Roosevelt Hotel (now the Fairmont) and in Arnaud's Restaurant.

Ellsworth Woodward (born in Seekonk, Maine, 1861; died in New Orleans, 1939) was an art teacher, painter, etcher, and sculptor who was active in New Orleans from 1885 to 1939. Dean of Newcomb Art School, he was identified for decades with art in New Orleans. At Newcomb, Woodward introduced the college's successful pottery program. He was president of the board of the Delgado Museum of Art. His special talent was watercolor painting, and he exhibited throughout his life at the Art Association. He did a mural decoration in the Criminal Courts Building at Broad Street and Tulane Avenue. William Woodward (born in Seekonk, Maine, 1859; died in New Orleans, 1939) was also known for portraits and landscapes. He painted ten portraits of former faculty members at Tulane, which hung in the faculty room.

Other artists who either lived in New Orleans in the twenties or made frequent visits to work here included George Castledon, who painted French Quarter courtyards and landscapes; Josephine Crawford, a self-taught artist who later studied art and held her first one-man show at the Arts and Crafts Club in 1928; Caroline Durieux, a lithographer, painter, etcher, and satirist who did caricatures as well as serious art; Gideon Stanton, a painter active in New Orleans from 1907 to 1950 who exhibited frequently at the New Orleans Art League and the Artists Guild; Helen Turner, a painter of portraits, landscapes, and still life, active in New Orleans from 1926 to 1949; and Ella Wood, a portrait painter, art teacher, and mural painter, active in New Orleans from 1911 to 1971.

In 1928, a group of Negro men formed the Little Arts and Crafts Club, and obtained instruction by mail. They gave three exhibits of their work, one at the Dryades Street Public Library, and two at the Negro Y.M.C.A.

Richard Barthe, a Negro sculptor, lived in New Orleans, where his modeling of small clay animals attracted the attention of a local critic. He studied at the Art Institute of Chicago and gained national recognition. He designed an eighty-foot frieze for a Negro auditorium in Harlem.

Gertrude Roberts Smith was known for her work at Newcomb with textiles and design; Inez Lugano for her miniatures; Sadie Irvine and Martha Westfeldt for their pottery; Anita Muras and Mary Butler for jewelry and silver. Sculptors of the period included Albert Rieker, Enrique Alferez, Angela Gregory, and Rai Graner Murray.

King Oliver's Creole Jazz Band (1923). Sitting, L to R: Baby Dodds, Honore Dutrey, Louis Armstrong, Johnny Dodds, and Lil Hardin (Louis Armstrong's second wife). Standing, L to R: King Oliver and Bill Johnson. (Courtesy Hogan Jazz Archives, Tulane University Library)

CHAPTER TWELVE

Music, Books, and Newspapers

*An ambivalent sense of exhilaration and foreboding permeates the novels
as well as the songs of the era.*
Arnold Shaw, *The Jazz Age*

WHEN WE THINK OF MUSIC in the twenties, we think of dancing, and dancing conjures up images of flailing arms, kicking legs, the Charleston, the fox-trot, dance marathons, short skirts, and gartered stockings. In New Orleans, the "hot" music of the twenties was jazz.

We call New Orleans the birthplace of jazz, though we can usually get an argument on that. Jazz first gained attention around the turn of the century, though its roots go back into history, and it grew and developed in the bawdy houses of Storyville in the teens.

In Storyville, the technical training of the downtown black Creole musicians and the raw-talent improvisations of the uptown black American musicians were forced to mix and soon gave birth to jazz. New tonalities were entering into the mainstream of popular music, and they would fix the sound of popular music for the next thirty years. In the twenties, what was happening was a joining of the elements of white music and black music, and the marriage would be firm and permanent.

Jazz played more than a minor role in building mutual respect and admiration between the races, who were forced to play together. "Piano keys opened doors to many white homes for black musicians," said Al Rose, author of *Storyville, New Orleans*.

Many New Orleans-born musicians, like "King" Oliver, Louis Armstrong, and Jelly Roll Morton, achieved fame in Chicago, New York, or on the West Coast in the twenties, after starting in Storyville in New Orleans.

Jazz (first spelled *jass*, a word whose origin was claimed by F. Scott Fitzgerald) almost instantaneously became a national craze. It had to be something revolutionary. Such a diversity of influences are reflected in jazz: white and Negro folk music, brass and military marches, and French tunes. "Tiger Rag" is said to be based on a French quadrille. The clarinet chorus of "High Society Blues" comes, supposedly, from a flute passage by John Philip Sousa. And Negro folk music can be heard in numerous "blues" songs like "Canal Street Blues," "Basin Street Blues," and "Milneburg Joys."

Jelly Roll Morton and his Red Hot Peppers (1926), L to R: Kid Ory, trombone; Andre Hillaire, drums; George Mitchell, trumpet; John Lindsay, bass; Jelly Roll Morton, piano; Johnny St. Cyr, banjo; and Omer Simeon, clarinet. (Courtesy Hogan Jazz Archives, Tulane University Library)

Jelly Roll Morton, the father of jazz and a musical genius, was born Ferdinand Joseph LaMenthe around 1885. His father was a black Creole, his stepfather a lower-class man. He never got over being "declassed." Being light-skinned, he passed for white much of the time. To avoid being called "Frenchy," he took his stepfather's name, Morton, and made up nicknames like "Winding Boy" and finally "Jelly Roll."

As a youth, he played piano in the luxurious bordellos of Storyville, making money in tips. He was thrown out of his grandmother's house (his grandmother raised him after his mother's death) because she feared he would be a bad influence on his sisters. He was a "hustler, pool shark, gambler, pimp, nightclub manager, entrepreneur, and high-liver," writes historian James Lincoln Collier, who also calls him "the first genius" in jazz.

Dan Morgenstern, of the Institute of Jazz Studies, adds, "It was Armstrong in the main who transformed the working repertory of the jazz musician from traditional materials . . . to great standards, drawn from the most fertile creative period of American songwriting."

Jelly Roll Morton was vain and arrogant. He made the claim, more than once, that he originated jazz. "It is evidently known," he said, "beyond contradiction, that New Orleans is the cradle of jazz, and I myself happen to be the creator in the year 1902." "Despite his boasting," Collier says, "he was fundamentally a decent man."

In Chicago, he made about 175 recordings, piano solos or piano "rolls" (for player pianos) of his own compositions. He later arranged and recorded originals like "Milneburg Joys," "Kansas City Stomps," and "Grandpa's Spells" with the famous Red Hot Peppers in 1926. Collier says, "It seems quite clear that Morton . . . showed Ellington, Henderson, Moten, Basie, Goodman and the rest, a way that jazz could go."

King Oliver, a trumpeter, played jazz in New Orleans till 1918 when he moved to Chicago, where his Creole Jazz Band, one of the greatest of the early and middle 1920s, played at the Lincoln Gardens. In this band, Louis Armstrong made his first appearance in the big time.

Louis ("Satchmo") Armstrong, the most famous of all jazzmen, was born in New Orleans in 1900. Living in a waifs' home, he began to play a cornet in a band there, and became the protégé of King Oliver. He is credited with being one of the world's great trumpeters, probably due to his way of leading or "crying up" to a note instead of just striking it decisively. He was also one of the first exponents of the "scat" style of singing. From the mid-1920s on, he had his own band. His bright, white smile, gravelly voice, and genial personality all combined to make him one of the most beloved performers in jazz.

"Kid" Ory (1886-1973), a New Orleans pioneer, began his music career by making a banjo out of a cigar box. At ten, he got a real banjo, and three years later was leading his own band at La Place, Louisiana, twenty-nine miles from New Orleans, which he visited on weekends to hear great players like Buddy Bolden. He moved to New Orleans, took up the trombone, and organized a band in which King Oliver played trumpet. When the "King" left for Chicago, "Satchmo" took his place. Ory moved to the West Coast, but three years later, in 1922, arrived in Chicago just before Louis Armstrong joined the historic King Oliver Band.

Ory recorded with Armstrong's "Hot Five" when they made their classic records for OKeh, including "Heebie Jeebies" in 1926 and "Muskrat Ramble."

Ory was a multitalented musician who performed on trombone, banjo, string bass, cornet, and alto sax. An interesting sidenote: he was known as a "tailgate" trombonist, the term derived from the practice in New Orleans of seating the trombone player at the far edge of the wagon on which the band rode, so that when they played, the trombonist could extend his slide for the low notes over the edge of the truck without striking the other players.

Johnny Dedroit was a well-known New Orleans jazzman of the twenties. He started playing trumpet solos at the age of twelve. His band included such well-known names in New Orleans music as Russ Papalia, Rudolph Levy, Henry Raymond, Frank Cuny, and Paul Dedroit. His band played in the "Cave" of the Grunewald Hotel (now the Fairmont), and had the distinction of being the first white band to play in tuxedos. They frequently played in Kolb's Restaurant and were much in demand for dances, hotels, and Carnival balls.

Oscar ("Papa") Celestin, venerable trumpet player and well-known New Orleans jazzman in the twenties, wrote "Marie Laveau" and "Down by the Riverside." He founded the original Tuxedo Brass Band.

Sweet Emma Barrett, "The Bell Gal," started in 1923 with Papa Celestin. A pianist and singer who earned her nickname by wearing belled garters, she in time had her own band and played with some of the city's top "reading" bands, although she couldn't read a note.

Bill Mathews (1889-1964) was a New Orleans jazz trombonist. He played with Jelly Roll Morton, the Original Tuxedo Orchestra, and Papa Celestin.

Clarence Williams, a pianist who was a swing virtuoso, went to New York and became a song publisher. He published "I Wish I Could Shimmy Like My Sister Kate," composed by A. J. Piron, who conducted an orchestra aboard the steamer *Capitol* out of New Orleans.

STEAMBOAT DANCIN' TO JAZZ

All throughout the twenties, steamboat riding with a special girl was a wonderful way for a young man to spend an evening or a Sunday afternoon. Dancing

Original Dixieland Jazz Band (1920), L to R: Tony Sbarbaro, Eddie Edwards, Nick LaRocca, Larry Shields, and Henry Ragas. (Courtesy Hogan Jazz Archives, Tulane University Library)

was the best part of the outing, and the bands hired by the Strekfus Steamboat Line (the *Sydney*, *J.S.*, *Capitol*, and *President*) were the finest jazz bands to be heard anywhere. One such band was led by a lady pianist, Fate Marable, whose organization included Baby Dodds, William ("Bebe") Ridgely, Joe Howard, Louis Armstrong, David Jones, Johnny Dodds, Johnny St. Cyr, and Pops Foster.

Other New Orleans Negro composers and exponents of jazz were Henry Allen, Jr., Buster Bailey, Sidney Bechet, Barney Bigard, Joe Oliver, and Spencer Williams.

Prominent white jazz artists were George Brunies, Eddie Edwards, Nick La-Rocca, Wingy Mannone, Henry Ragas, Leon Rappolo, Larry Shields, and Tony Sbarbaro. Louis Prima, another New Orleans singer and musician, won wide renown on radio, the Broadway stage, and in moving pictures.

NEW ORLEANS, A FOUNTAINHEAD OF INSPIRATION FOR WRITERS

New Orleans, surrounded by steamy swamps abounding with snakes and alligators, has been called exotic, moody, spooky, enchanted, and romantic. Every adjective applies. It is a city with more European flavor than any other in America. With its history of hurricanes, floods, and fevers, and its cast of heroic historic characters, its above-ground cities of the dead, its diverse ethnic population, jazz culture and legendary food, it has provided the settings for thousands of stories in the Romantic mode. For any gifted writer, living in New Orleans means being surrounded by the richest, most fascinating settings in the world. It also means being a part of a literary scene both past and present that is unsurpassed in any other city.

New Orleans has experienced two periods of great literary outpourings, and at the present time, even as you read, it may be entering a third. The first great Renaissance was the period of the 1880s and 1890s; the second was in the 1920s.

The event that triggered the first Renaissance was the World's Fair and Cotton Centennial Exposition of 1884, held in what is now Audubon Park. To cover this event, publishers and writers came to the city and stayed for six months, sending daily reports to New York newspapers and magazines like *Scribner's*, *Century*, and *Harper's*. These publishers and writers entered into the life of the city and assisted promising but obscure young writers like Lafcadio Hearn, George Washington Cable, and Grace King in securing recognition.

Beginning her career toward the end of the first literary Renaissance and continuing it well into the 1920s was a writer called Dorothy Dix (real name Elizabeth Merriwether Gilmer). She was recuperating on the Gulf Coast when she met the owner of the *Picayune* and sold her first story to that paper for three dollars. Shortly thereafter, in 1896, she arrived in New Orleans and joined the staff of the *Picayune*, where she began writing articles for women. By 1920, she was the highest-paid woman writer in the world, and her advice to the lovelorn was carried in newspapers all over the globe.

THE SECOND LITERARY RENAISSANCE: THE 1920s

The catalyst of the blossoming of literature in New Orleans in the 1920s was a small literary magazine called *The Double Dealer*, which was founded in January 1921 by a group of intellectuals including John McClure (the literary editor of the *Times-Picayune* in the twenties), Basil Thompson, Julius Friend, Albert Goldstein, Flo Field, Richard Kirk, Louis Gilmore, and James Feibleman. It published the works of Robert Penn Warren, Sherwood Anderson, William Faulkner, Ezra Pound, Thornton Wilder, Allen Tate, Ernest Hemingway, and others. The founders of this magazine had returned from World War I without any idea of what to do with their lives. They also wanted to refute the statement of H. L. Mencken, who had said that the South was a cultural Sahara. They wanted to break with the old literary traditions and try something new. Their magazine was cosmopolitan, antipuritanical, and liberal.

Their first issue declared: "To myopics, we desire to indicate the hills; to visionaries, the unwashed dishes. . . . We mean to deal double, to show the other side, to throw open the back windows stuck in their sills from misuse, smutted over long since against even a dim beam's penetration." These were strong words in New Orleans, where literature had followed the Romantic tradition for the past hundred years. The magazine was devoted to literature, poetry, and literary criticism. It represented both radical and conservative movements in literature in the 1920s.

The magazine lasted only five and a half years, but many of the contributing writers stayed on in New Orleans. To them, the Vieux Carré was kind of a Left-Bank Paris, which attracted struggling artists and writers. They revelled in the picturesque atmosphere of decaying old buildings, and found the low rents helpful.

In the twenties, William Faulkner, a native Mississippian who had been in New Orleans for a while, decided that this is where he would stay and write. He'd arrived in New Orleans with a coat filled with bottles of whiskey, but no money. He hocked everything he owned, including a typewriter that wasn't his. Hard times nurtured his creativity, as it did many another artist's, whose talent seemed to require a certain amount of poverty, and the Vieux Carré in the twenties, with its crumbling buildings, was the place to find it.

Among his friends and drinking buddies was a celebrated author named Sherwood Anderson, who had declared that New Orleans was the only place fit to be an artist's home. He lived in New Orleans from 1922 to 1925 in the deteriorating Pontalba Apartments, and was the leader of the creative forces in local literature and a contributor to *The Double Dealer*. He wrote the novel *Many Marriages*.

Faulkner and Anderson used to walk around together and sit drinking and talking until three or four in the morning. Faulkner said of Anderson, "He never did any work, that I could see. Looking at Anderson, I thought to myself, 'Being a writer must be a wonderful life.'" With that thought in mind, Faulkner vanished into his apartment on Pirates' Alley in 1924 and emerged in six weeks with his first novel, *Soldier's Pay*. In later years, when Faulkner had moved away, he often returned to New Orleans for inspiration or just to have fun. He was later to win both the Nobel prize for literature and two Pulitzer prizes for his novels *A Fable* and *The Reivers*.

In his novels, he developed the "stream of consciousness" technique, borrowed partly from James Joyce. His works include *The Sound and the Fury, As I Lay Dying*, and *Absalom, Absalom!*

The first book released by Pelican Publishing Company, founded in 1926 by Stuart Landry, was Faulkner's first trade paperback, *Sherwood Anderson and Other Famous Creoles*. The personalities in the book were some of the people who frequented the Pelican Book Shop, an important gathering place for New Orleans

literary people in the twenties. It is possible that Landry and McClure named the
publishing company after the Pelican Book Shop.

Lyle Saxon, a native of Louisiana and a resident of New Orleans for over
twenty years who had served his apprenticeship in newspaper work with the
Times-Picayune, was another novelist of the twenties and thirties. He died in
1946, having produced many books about New Orleans and environs, including
Fabulous New Orleans (1928), *Old Louisiana* (1929), *Lafitte the Pirate* (1930), and
Children of Strangers (1937).

*Lyle Saxon, popular novelist, was a native of Louisiana and a resident of New Orleans in the
twenties. His books include* Fabulous New Orleans *(1928) and* Old Louisiana *(1929). In the
1930s, he was the state director of the Federal Writers' Project for the WPA New Orleans City
Guide. Saxon died in 1946.*

Saxon portrayed New Orleans in a way that made other writers want to come and write here. In the twenties and beyond, his dwelling became a literary salon of sorts. He was later selected as state director of the WPA Writers' Project, which produced the *New Orleans City Guide,* the *Louisiana State Guide,* and *Gumbo Ya-Ya.*

Lyle Saxon, I'm proud to say, was a close friend of my aunt and uncle, Charles and Hazel Dahlin, to whom he personalized several of his novels, books which are now on my bookshelves. My uncle (by marriage) was a Swede; he was a wonderful drinking buddy and a good listener, the kind of friend all writers need. Together, Charlie and Lyle spent many an hour at Kolb's Restaurant, talking books and paintings. Another of my uncle's friends was an artist, George Izvolsky, whom I was happy to find listed among outstanding local artists in the *New Orleans City Guide.*

Roark Bradford, who lived off and on in the city in the twenties and thirties, first came to New Orleans to do newspaper work. An early short story, "Child of God," won him the O. Henry Memorial Award for 1927. He soon became widely known for this and for "Ol' Man Adam an' His Chillun." He knew the blacks of the South perhaps better than anyone else writing at that time, and used the plantations of Louisiana and Mississippi for his background.

In the 1920s, F. Scott Fitzgerald came to New Orleans and lived for a while in a boardinghouse at 2900 Prytania Street while he was reading galley proofs of *This Side of Paradise.* New Orleans likes to claim Fitzgerald, but actually he was only passing through. He liked jazz, champagne, and laziness, which made him much like Faulkner, but after staying here for a while, he left for Europe, where he became the image of the expatriate American in the 1920s.

Hermann B. Deutsch, well-known New Orleans journalist, wrote numerous articles and stories, some appearing in *Esquire* and *The Saturday Evening Post.* His first book, a biography of Gen. Lee Christmas (1931), was set partly in New Orleans.

Robert Emmet Kennedy, a native of Gretna, in his short stories "Black Cameos" (1924) and "Gritny People" (1927) and his novel, *Red Bean Row* (1929), became known as a gifted writer dealing with Negro life.

Charles Tenney Jackson married Carlotta Weir of New Orleans and spent a lot of time in the city just before the twenties. In *Captain Sazerac* (1922), he used the historical background of New Orleans in a novel about the Lafitte pirates.

Quiet Cities (1928) and *Swords and Roses* (1929) by Joseph Hergesheimer are laid partly in New Orleans, the second title an interesting study of the Southern general P. G. T. Beauregard.

Oliver LaFarge wrote *Laughing Boy,* which won him the 1930 Pulitzer Prize. He spent two years in New Orleans (1926-28) as assistant in ethnology at Tulane University.

Carl Carmer spent two years in the city, working as a columnist on the *Morning Tribune.* He wrote *French Town* (1928) and is best known for *Stars Fell on Alabama.*

Harris Dickson, a Mississippi author, wrote extensively of New Orleans in newspapers and magazines and published three novels, including *Children of the River* (1928).

NEWSPAPERS IN NEW ORLEANS

The most important newspapers published in New Orleans in the 1920s were the *Times-Picayune,* the *Item,* the *States,* and the *Morning Tribune.*

The Times-Picayune Publishing Company building faced Lafayette Square in 1924. This picture was taken from St. Patrick's Church on Camp Street. Note the Hibernia Bank tower, left rear, the highest building in the city. (Courtesy Times-Picayune Publishing Company)

The *Times-Picayune* was the result of journalistic development in Louisiana that took a century. The *Picayune*, established in 1837, was so called because it sold for a picayune, the smallest coin currently in use. The *New Orleans Times* absorbed the *Crescent* in 1868 and later combined with the *Democrat* to form the *Times-Democrat* in 1881, which merged with the *Picayune* in 1914 to form the *Times-Picayune.*

The New Orleans *Item*, founded in 1877, was said to be the oldest afternoon newspaper in the South. The *States* was an evening daily formed in 1880, owned and published by the Times-Picayune Publishing Company. The *Morning Tribune*, established in 1924, was later a tabloid published by the *Item*. Besides these, there were more than forty other news publications issued weekly, monthly, or quarterly in the city.

St. Stephen's graduating class of 1921. The school was in the 900 block of Napoleon Avenue, later the site of apartment houses. St. Stephen's Elementary School was in the 1000 block with the church. L to R: Eliskadell Bates, Elise Soniat, Ernestine Palmer, Margaret Flynn, Marie Carroll, Ruth Nutter, Bessie Bursch, Lillian Boudreaux, and contributor's mother, Mary Schiele, later Belsom. The building was demolished in 1966. (Courtesy Jack Belsom)

CHAPTER THIRTEEN

Fads and Fashions: The Decadent Decade

The parties were bigger. The pace was faster, the shows were broader, the buildings were higher, the morals were looser, and the liquor was cheaper; but all these profits did not minister to much delight.

F. Scott Fitzgerald

WHEN IN THE HISTORY of the world did upheaval not begin with the young? Even Socrates wrote a treatise on rebellious youth that could be taken as an editorial written in the *Times-Picayune* about the youth of the 1990s.

Collegians of the twenties, as if they were the first generation to resent the state of the world and to blame it on their parents, were changing American morals and conduct. The typical college male toted a flask on his hip, played his ukelele, and slicked back his hair like Valentino. The typical female dispensed with her girdle; wore her hair bobbed, her skirts short, her stockings sheer; and experimented with liquor and cigarettes. Collegians were worldly. They were sophisticates. They disdained social convention.

The irony of it was that they adhered fiercely to many traditions of past collegians. The twenties saw the heyday of the Greek fraternities. College kids turned out in a body for football rallies and games. At LSU, hundreds of students turned out daily at the stadium just to watch football practice. Yet there were drinking binges and speeding drivers taking coeds out to rowdy roadhouses to "crash" parties. Automobile accidents were frequent.

College dances were wild. "Cutting in," which was considered daring, originated in the South, but soon moved to the North. Girls with good figures and flirty manners were "cut in on" the most. This encouraged all girls to dress and talk like "flappers." If this was what boys wanted, this is what they'd get.

Some small schools, especially those run by religious orders, had dress codes: "Thin dress material may be used provided suitable underslips are worn," said Northwest Nazarene College of Nampa, Idaho. "Skirts must . . . not expose the calf of the leg. . . ." Yet many campuses in time abolished dress codes, cancelled compulsory chapel attendance, permitted smoking for women, and winked at drinking parties.

THE FREEWHEELING DECADE

More than anything else, young people craved excitement. They loved the tabloids with their gory murders, the world championship boxing matches, the visits of celebrities like Lindbergh to the Crescent City.

Hedonism fed on itself, and when Prohibition became law in 1919, the simple
pleasure of sipping a drink became a crime, and opened up a whole new vista of
derring-do: flasks on the hip and under the garter, dark entryways to speakeasies
in the Quarter, and homemade gin and beer.

Prohibition and movies made the decade decadent. Movies like *Our Dancing
Daughters,* with Joan Crawford, showed young people how glamorous it was to
drink and neck and do all the sensual dances like the tango and the Charleston
and the fox-trot. Movie stars did these things, and they were the role models of
the young. Parents shook their heads in despair.

Billboards advertising the Crawford movie and its sequel promised "brilliant
men, beautiful jazz babies, champagne baths, midnight revels, petting parties in
the purple dawn . . ." and on and on. And Crawford wasn't alone. There was
Theda Bara, the "vamp"; Clara Bow, the "It" girl; and Garbo, who "vanted to be
alone," but seldom was.

BE LIKE EVERYONE ELSE, AND STILL BE DIFFERENT

This was possible in the twenties. If you took up one of the zany fads sweeping
the country, you became a conformist; if you did it *better* than anyone else, you
became a hero.

The world of radio and syndicated columns spread pop culture across the country almost overnight. Nothing was gradual. Beauty contests, crossword puzzles,
flagpole sitting, mah-jongg, marathon running, marathon dancing, contract
bridge, yo-yos, roller skating, rocking chair derbies, champion pea-eaters, kissers,
and talkers were all applauded, admired, and imitated. One high school student
put forty sticks of chewing gum in his mouth, sang "Home, Sweet Home," and
between verses, drank a gallon of milk.

Beauty contests began with the Miss America contest in Atlantic City in 1921.
It started as a gag, a scheme to get tourists to stay in Atlantic City after Labor
Day. The "Cinderella" theme was appealing. Promoters promised to take an or-
dinary, good-looking girl and turn her into a celebrity.

In the first contest, only eight girls competed. By 1927, the festivities had become a week-long schedule of exhausting competitions.

Crossword puzzles became the rage when two young publishers, Richard Simon
and M. Lincoln Schuster, brought out a collection of puzzles as their first book.
They advertised it widely, and suddenly, it was "in." College teams competed in
tournaments.

Slang was a sign of sophistication. A girl called her boyfriend her "sheik." He
called her his "sheba." "Hooch" and "giggle-water" meant liquor. When you
agreed with someone emphatically, you said, "And *how!*" or "I should hope to tell
you!" A plain girl was a "jane." A beauty was "the cat's meow," the "bee's knees,"
and "the berries."

If a girl danced on top of a table at a fraternity party, the sheiks might gather
'round and yell, "Get hot!" If a girl wished to get rid of a bore, she might tell him,
"Go fly a kite," or "Go cook a radish."

"I love my wife but oh, you kid!" is self-explanatory. "All wet" meant wrong,
mistaken. "Applesauce" meant nonsense, as did baloney, bunk, banana oil, ho-
kum, and horsefeathers. A "big cheese" was an important person. A "bull ses-
sion" was a group discussion. To "bump off" was to murder. To "carry a torch" was

to suffer from unrequited love. "Cheaters" were eyeglasses. A "gam" was a girl's leg.

The words gin mill, gold digger, goofy, gyp, hard-boiled, heebie-jeebies, hep, and high-hat were all new in the twenties, but no explanation is needed for them today. I think we can also understand if everything's jake, hotsy-totsy, or keen.

Flagpole sitting was a way of attracting attention. Alvin ("Shipwreck") Kelly was the decade's most famous flagpole sitter. He started his hijinks in Hollywood in 1924, where a studio had hired him to draw a crowd. Soon he was being hired by hotels that were trying to attract crowds. He balanced himself on a small disk atop a pole, placing his feet in stirrups so as not to fall off. He took catnaps of five minutes every hour, and subsisted on liquids lifted up to him.

In March of 1928, he climbed atop the flagpole at the Jung Hotel at 1500 Canal Street, hoping to stay aloft for 100 hours, thus breaking his own record. He remained awake till the third night, when a rainstorm with high winds forced him down after only 80 hours.

Alvin ("Shipwreck") Kelly, the famous flagpole sitter of the twenties, came to New Orleans on several occasions. Here, atop a flagpole at the Jung Hotel, he said he'd stay for 100 hours, but was forced by weather to come down after 80. (Courtesy Times-Picayune Publishing Company)

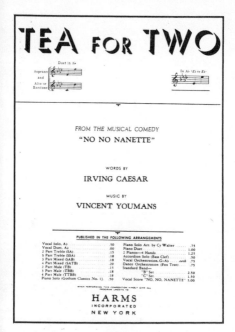

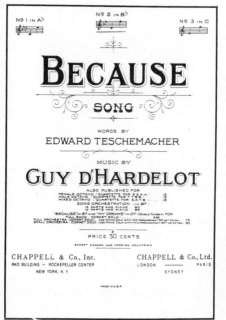

MAH-JONGG HITS AMERICA

In 1922, an ancient Chinese game called mah-jongg became popular in the U.S. Within a year, millions of people, mostly ladies, were playing it. And many refused to play unless dressed in Chinese kimonos.

Mah-jongg gave popularity to the kimono style of the twenties. My Aunt Hazel, then a young single lady in her twenties, had mah-jongg games in her parlor. She bought a Chinese buddha for her mantel, inside which she burned incense while the games were in progress.

The game of mah-jongg required both dice and dominos. It consisted of a set of 144 tiles made of the shinbones of calves. A good set made in China could cost $500, but soon, enterprising Americans were making copies that sold for $2 or $3. The rules of the game were complicated, and every rule book differed from every other.

YOWSAH, YOWSAH, YOWSAH! THE MARATHON DANCE IS ABOUT TO BEGIN!

This was the call of the promoter who started off the craziest competition of all, the Marathon Dance. The object of the dance was to see which couple could outdance all the others, and manage to come out alive at the end.

Couples competed for prizes of one or two thousand dollars, and spectators paid to come in and see them perform for eight or nine days, or as long as it took them to quit or have heart attacks. To keep their partners awake, dancers pinched them or kicked them or even dropped them into a tub of ice water. (Remember *They Shoot Horses, Don't They?*) To get rid of their competition, dancers sometimes put sleeping pills or laxatives into their drinks. Of all the competitions popular in the twenties, none was more cruel than the dance marathon.

CLOSE DANCING, HOT MUSIC, AND SILLY SONGS

"Don't play that horrible music so loud!" Parents said it in the twenties, the thirties, the forties, and in every decade and every generation. But the youth of the twenties were the first to have radios to play their wild, frenetic songs with crazy nonsensical lyrics.

Puritanical older generations considered any kind of "close" dancing the first step on the road to degredation. They thought it cheapened women. Any girl who would let a man put his arm around her and swing her around was not a "nice" girl. But the "twenties" girl was a whole new breed. She was wild and worldly and sophisticated, and she gladly did the "Black Bottom," the "shimmy," and the Charleston when the bands played jazzy numbers. To slow music, she did the fox-trot or the two-step, but "close" dancing was here to stay, and there was nothing Mama could do about it.

Crazy lyrics captured the essence of the decade. Songs like "Runnin' wild, lost control, runnin' wild, mighty bold . . ." or "If you knew Susie like I know Susie, Oh! Oh! Oh, what a gal!" caught on, and people sang them everywhere. Many beautiful songs came out of the decade, however, like George Gershwin's "Lady Be Good," "The Man I Love," and "Someone to Watch Over Me."

160

"Dress-up" clothes of the decade made young women look old. No lady was considered "dressed" without a cloche hat, and since the snug-fitting hat allowed no room for hair, the coiffures were all short. They might be as straight and shingled as a man's hair or as crimpy and curly as Joan Crawford's, but they were short.

Dresses were straight and shapeless, designed to flatten the bosom and give the overall "sheath" effect. Overcoats were dress length and equally shapeless, with fur collars and sometimes fur cuffs. Separate stone marten furs were sometimes worn over a cloth coat. Women wore stockings, that went without saying, and shoes were usually sandals with medium heels or oxfords with Cuban heels.

"Our Sweetheart" of McDonogh Thirty-Five in 1929 was Mae Felicie Rogers. In 1917, the school had changed from an elementary Negro school to a High and Normal school, adding one grade and dropping one grade each year. The Teachers' Course was added in 1924. (Courtesy Ann M. Novakov)

At three years old, Mildred Laguens was the flower girl at the wedding of Will and Sarah Koenig in 1924. (Courtesy Lynette Vinet)

Frank Datri was groomsman in Tony Miceli's wedding at the Cathedral in 1920. Here he is in white tie, tails, gloves, and boutonniere. (Courtesy Ann M. Novakov)

The wedding of Dorothy Rose Navo and James Elliot Harrison, Sr., took place on June 16, 1926 at St. Joseph's Church on Tulane Avenue. The couple resided for many years in the New Orleans and Hammond areas, and today their many descendants live throughout southeastern Louisiana. (Courtesy Byron James Elliot Hoover)

Charlotte Bianchina Scurria and husband Salvador had their picture taken on Chartres Street in 1920. She holds her umbrella and his campaign hat. He holds her. (Courtesy Judy Pesses)

Hazel Schultis (later Dahlin), author's aunt, at twenty-three years old in 1921. She was a public school teacher for forty years, most of them at John McDonogh High.

Giovanni Datri, an immigrant from Palermo, Sicily, as he looked in the mid-twenties, with handlebar moustache, flamboyant tie, watch chain, and boutonniere. (Courtesy Ann M. Novakov)

Employees of A. Bladwin & Co., wholesale hardware dealers, pose for a company photo October 6, 1923 in Jackson Square. Contributor's father, Ernest Andre Haro, salesman, is in the top row, ninth from right. (Courtesy Germaine Widmer)

Ladies' Home Journal and *Collier's* magazines showed "dressy" dresses with the long, lean look, designed to make the bust flat and boyish looking, and the bodice long-waisted and belted at the hip, with no discernible indentation at the waist. Necklines could be collarless in the boat-neck design or ornamented with shawl collars, scarves, pleated ties, or flowers.

Dresses were made distinctive by the addition of a capelet of the same fabric, inverted pleats in the skirt, or a bolero of matching or contrasting fabric. Fabrics popular in the twenties were silk crepe, crepe de chine, and wool crepe. Dress hems were made in handkerchief style, the corners of the hankies pointing floorward. Long-waisted dresses were adorned with lace or embroidered appliqués or sometimes a large silk rose at the line where the bodice met the skirt.

Hats came in five outstanding materials: ballibuntl, sangha straw, perle Visca, crin, and felt for the spring season. With warmer weather, larger, lighter hats were worn. The folded or draped crown of the cloche, with or without a brim, was all the rage. Brown in all its shades was the favorite color for millinery of the

& COMPANY.

middle twenties, followed by *bois de rose,* green, chartreuse, scarlet, blue, white, and pastels. The rule for trimming on hats was "the less, the better."

By the end of the decade, cloches were becoming stovepipes or featured added rolled brims. Women were looking for a softer look. In 1930, the wide-brimmed picture hat emerged.

Dress shoes were of leather, kid, patent leather, and suede, but animal skins were high fashion: alligator, lizard, snake, chameleon, baby leopard, and shark. Dress shoes had higher heels than ever before—two and five-eighths inches was not out of the ordinary. Styles included pumps, dressy high-vamped sports ox-fords, and high-heeled sandals with double or triple straps.

The hat, frock, and shoes had to harmonize. The key word was *ensemble.* But with color and material in endless varieties—with handbags, handkerchiefs, scarves, flowers, and all the other small accessories available—coordinating one's costume was a fascinating task.

Desdemona Grace (now Mrs. Albert M. Redlich of Mandeville) and the late Dr. George J. Doody, a 1929 Loyola dentistry graduate, took a "daring duo" stance atop Marquette Hall at Loyola in 1927. (Courtesy Rev. Thomas Clancy, S.J. and Loyola University)

Young Women's Organization of Loyola in 1927. With cloche hats and fur collars, the ladies gathered on the lawn behind Marquette Hall. (Courtesy Loyola University)

Remember bloomers? You're giving away your age if you say yes. I recall wearing them as a small child in the thirties. We wore woolen bloomers under our Catholic school uniform skirts for warmth in the wintertime. To bring it even closer to date, we wore black gym bloomers at Holy Angels Academy in the forties, and they had to be pulled down to cover the roll garters of our mandatory stockings. But by the forties, stylish ladies had long since abandoned the loose fitting underpants with the elasticized waist and legs.

Bloomers in the twenties were worn with vests, which were no-frill camisole tops, made of cotton or silk, with a band across the top of the bust, and wide straps. Step-ins were wide-legged panties, called "tap pants" today. Also in vogue were princess slips, nightgowns, pajamas, and union suits. Union suits were long woolen underwear that came as separates or as all-in-one long johns. Neither of these were seen very often in the hot Crescent City.

Another fact that needs mention is that women didn't wear slacks in the twenties, unless they were Greta Garbo, and who was—or wanted to be?

All of these items of underwear could be purchased at Feibleman's on Canal and Carondelet or at Rougelot's on Esplanade and Frenchmen. My Memere wore chemises till she died in the 1940s. By the forties, she could no longer buy them ready-made. She had to buy the fabric and have them made. These were wide-strapped, straight-lined cotton slips without a decoration of any kind.

JEWELRY AND COIFFURES

Jewelry consisted of long pearls, two or three strands that hung almost to the waist; pierced or clip-on earrings; diamond bar pins (whose purpose, apart from decoration, was to keep the dress and undergarments securely held together); encased watches that hung from pins; wristwatches; rings; and multistrand pearl chokers.

Helen Marie Abadie, a young New Orleans beauty of 1922, wears a straw boater, a chiffon dress edged with braid, and a string of pearls to have her picture taken. (Courtesy Bill Gallmann, Jr.)

Loyola coeds. Top L to R: Araguel, Beaud, and Dodge. Second row: Dunn, Grace, Mott, and Pilsbury. Third row: Raynes, Roach, and Salatich. Fourth row: Taylor, Turcy, and Weilbacher. (Courtesy Loyola University)

Miss Violet Loretta Irwin (later Mrs. John S. Burke) was thrilled with her fashionable new hairdo in 1925. We might have giggled at it in the forties, but it's back again in the nineties. (Courtesy John S. Burke, Jr.)

Coiffures were mainly short, but there were a few holdouts who wore a bun at the neck and finger waves on the crown of the head. Some hairstyles were exactly like men's: parted, slicked back, and shingled. This extremely short style came out in 1926 and was known as the "Eton crop." In a variation of this style, a "spit curl" in front of the ear or bangs on the forehead might be worn to soften the severity of the hairdo.

One style of "bob" had a center part, bangs, and hair combed snugly to the head with tiny curls over the ears. Another "bob" slicked down to the head, and was cut exactly at the hairline, except for the hair over the ears, which was left two or three inches longer, so as to make a bouquet of curls over each ear. A longer hairdo was swept back, partly covering the ears, and caught at the nape with a barrette. The ends were arranged in a single soft swirling curl.

Hair adornments might be artificial plaits of hair kept in place by a narrow headband, or a Spanish comb tucked into a bun at the nape of the neck. Those who wore their hair long wore it smooth and close to the head.

By 1929, the shingle was worn a little longer, and the back hair was often long enough to be rolled into a bun, with roll curls or small flat pin curls at the nape of the neck.

Ladies protected their hairstyles overnight with Lorraine silk hair nets with elastic edges, which could be purchased at Woolworth's for five cents.

The choice retail block of the South, the 900 block of Canal Street, downtown side. L to R: the Audubon Building with its many stores and offices, Kress Co., and the Maison Blanche Building. Cars were allowed angle parking on Canal Street in the twenties.

CHAPTER FOURTEEN

The Grand Old Stores

Silks and satins and ribbon that shows,
And I'll be yours in buttons and bows.

OF ALL THE CANAL STREET STORES that New Orleanians frequented in the twenties, and for decades before and after, Maison Blanche and Krauss are the last two still in business. The emporiums that had their glory days in the twenties and after were Maison Blanche, D. H. Holmes, Godchaux, and Krauss. These were the fine old retail stores of Canal Street. In their day, they were more than just places that sold goods. They were institutions.

MAISON BLANCHE

The new Christ Church, at the corner of Canal and Dauphine streets, was torn down in 1886, to be replaced by the Mercier Building, which in turn was torn down in 1906 to be replaced by the Maison Blanche Building. And Maison Blanche, despite time and the depressed economy, still does business at the same old stand.

Everyone shopped at Maison Blanche in the twenties and thirties and in later decades. It was established at its present location, 901 Canal Street, as a quality store with moderate prices. And that has never changed. Maison Blanche was not just a seller of merchandise. Its promotion was unexcelled. Over the years, even in the twenties, it offered fashion shows and festivals, glamor, entertainment, fantasy, and show-biz celebrities, to rival in brilliance even the movie palaces of the city.

In the twenties, my mother, then a teenager and later a young wife and mother, bought her fabrics and notions there for sewing, as well as kitchen utensils and gifts.

In the twenties, there was an arcade just inside the front doors, and beyond the arcade, against the front wall, was the glove department with its lineup of wooden seats, where a lady could sit to try on a pair of kid gloves. Treating a customer like a queen, the saleslady sprinkled powder into the glove to prevent the hand from sticking to the buttery fabric.

The millinery department was fitted out with dressing tables with three-way looking glasses. When Mother went there to choose a hat, a saleslady selected a

Maison Blanche Department Store, built in 1909 on the corner of Canal and Dauphine streets, with its terra-cotta and marble facade. This is how it looked in the twenties.

173

becoming picture hat and placed it on her head at just the right angle. Then, with a hand mirror, Mother carefully examined its fit and flattery.

The notions department, now of fond memory, was a seamstress's dream with its infinite variety of needles, pins, buttons, thread, and embroidery accessories.

Maison Blanche was a locally owned store, founded by Isadore Newman and passed down to his sons, Edgar and J. K. Newman, who founded the City Stores chain in 1920. Though the chain owned the store, the chain was established by the same family that started the store; therefore, the store was said to be locally owned.

D. H. HOLMES

D. H. Holmes, the oldest of the downtown emporiums, was founded in 1842. Daniel Henry Holmes, then twenty-six, established his first store on Chartres Street and moved in 1849 to 819 Canal. He opened a "department store" when it was a brand new concept.

In 1913, the building was remodeled and the facade changed from a Gothic to a neoclassic look, with multiple windows across the front. At street level was a wide marquee, beneath which the famous Holmes clock was centered. This was the facade familiar to shoppers in the twenties.

At Christmas, it was a tradition in my mother's time (the twenties) and in mine (the thirties) to go see the D. H. Holmes window with its extravagantly decorated sets filled with dozens of costumed, mechanical miniature characters.

In 1989, Dillard Department Stores, Inc. of Little Rock, Arkansas took over the whole chain of D. H. Holmes stores. The store at 819 Canal Street closed that year, and the historic building was donated by the Dillard's chain to the city. Plans are under consideration to restore the neoclassic facade of the twenties. The use to which the building will be put is still undecided.

Stores in the 800 block of Canal Street included D. H. Holmes (white store with awning, center). Note crescent in the river to rear of picture.

Holmes Restaurant, a popular dining area for working people and shoppers in D. H. Holmes Department Store, the twenties.

The Don Chase Orchestra played daily to entertain diners in Holmes Restaurant.

GODCHAUX'S

Across the street from D. H. Holmes, Godchaux's, with its ornate Canal Street facade and its architecturally embellished arcade of display windows, gave off an air of exclusiveness. It opened at its Canal Street location in 1926. In later decades, it was the flagship store for several suburban branch stores and others in Houma and on the Gulf Coast. In 1980, it was one of the oldest department stores, if not *the* oldest department store, in the United States still owned by descendants of the founder. Third, fourth, and fifth generation Godchauxs still worked in the store on Canal Street until it closed in 1985.

In 1926, the store added women's clothing to its inventory. It evolved into a "classy" department store, selling men's, women's, and children's clothing, as well as perfume, jewelry, gifts, and home accessories. In 1980, the Godchaux's stores were still thriving. Today, they are gone.

A merchant who left home to make his fortune was Leon Heymann. In 1900, at seventeen, he left New Orleans for rural South Louisiana where he established several junior department stores. In 1920, he returned to New Orleans, where he married Thekla Krauss and took over the controlling interest in Krauss Department Store at 1201 Canal Street.

In 1920, shortly before the founder, Leon Fellman, died, Heymann bought his share of Krauss Company, and he and his wife's brothers (the four Krauss brothers) then bought up the shares of minority stockholders, making it a family business.

Unlike the other downtown emporiums that promoted sales with glamorous programs, Krauss always took a more down-to-earth approach, offering such things as sewing clinics and business seminars.

Times change but Krauss remains the same. Its Canal Street facade (except for being larger) looks pretty much the way it did in the twenties. The original structure, which comprised about a fifth of a block, grew over the years to a two-block building.

Krauss still uses pneumatic tubes for sales transactions involving Krauss credit cards and it's not just to keep things "old-fashioned" looking. It is also fast and efficient. According to Manager John Cecil, the tube takes the credit card and sales slip to the Tube Room, where a computer monitor calls up the customer's account number and approves the sale. The receipt is then returned to the department.

The mezzanine is timeless, and so is the dining area on the mezzanine. Orleanians like things to stay the same. It gives them an anchored feeling, a feeling of security, a confidence that all of New Orleans is not slipping away from them. Krauss gives that to its customers. It stays in the same place, its salespeople offering customers the same kind of old-world courtesy they offered in the twenties, their manners echoing the old adage that the customer is always right.

SPECIALTY STORES

Three other stores are worthy of mention not only because they fronted on Canal Street in the twenties but because of their longevity in the same location.

Adler's jewelry store was built in 1908 and came to occupy 718-20 and 722 Canal Street. Coleman Adler founded the store in 1897. The name Adler has come to be synonymous with fine jewelry in New Orleans. Adler's is another store that still uses pneumatic tubes in sales transactions.

Werlein's Music Store, in the 600 block of Canal Street, occupied a building erected in the first decade of the century, with elaborate glazed terra-cotta ornamentation. The second-story window treatment is an elliptical arch. Werlein's sold all kinds of musical instruments, sheet music, and popular recordings in the twenties. Private rooms allowed a customer to listen to a record before purchasing it. My piano teacher, Miss Alice Gascon, held her piano recitals in a small auditorium on Werlein's second floor in the twenties and the thirties. The Canal Street property is today the Palace Cafe. Werlein's now has music stores on Veterans Highway, on Decatur Street, and on the West Bank in Gretna.

Kress Five-and-Dime was built in 1910 on the lake side of Maison Blanche.

THE TERRACE, 828 CANAL ST.
Fuerst & Kraemer
LIMITED
NEW ORLEANS, LA.

The Terrace Room of Fuerst and Kraemer, 828 Canal Street. Working people and shoppers stopped for lunch or a snack there in the twenties. Author's mother lunched there when she worked for Pan-American Life Insurance Company, 1920-24.

Only three buildings occupied the 900 block of Canal Street at that time: Maison Blanche, Kress, and the Audubon Building. Kress was part of a chain and was the largest Kress store in the country. In the twenties, it had a fine terra-cotta facade. The entryway was an open arcade floored with mosaic tile and flanked by huge display windows. Kress offered notions, toys, kitchen utensils, underwear, plants, candy, and hardware. Also very popular was its lunch counter and soda fountain.

In 1791, Spanish authorities put a good solid roof on the French Market building, located along the riverfront near Jackson Square, at the site of the present-day market. Trucks and mule-drawn wagons brought produce from nearby truck farms. The original building was destroyed in 1812, replaced with an arcaded structure in 1813, and an addition was put on in 1823. The market had more than one hundred stalls.

CHAPTER FIFTEEN

To Market, to Market

*Quartee beans, quartee rice, little piece of salt meat to make it taste
nice. Lend me the paper, and tell me the time. When Papa passes by,
he'll pay you the dime.*

EVERY DAY WAS MARKET DAY in the twenties, since refrigeration was largely dependent on the old wooden icebox. But French Quarter residents always did a special shopping on Sunday mornings, my father recalled in his memoirs. For generations before the 1920s, natives went to the French Market after breakfast on Sundays to "make groceries." This expression probably grew out of our French culture, in which the verb *faire* means *to do* or *make.* Today, young people say, "I'm going to 'do' my grocery shopping." For those who learned French as a first language, the translation came out, "I'm going to 'make' groceries."

After early Mass on Sundays, which Daddy's family always attended (fasting from midnight to receive Communion made it difficult to go to late Mass), they'd return home to a huge breakfast that had been prepared in their absence by their Negro cook. Afterwards, my grandmother and her servant, with a basket on her arm, went to market.

THE FRENCH MARKET OF THE 1920s

Approaching the French Market, shoppers first saw trucks and wagons laden with meat, fish, and poultry lined up at the stalls. Once past the traffic congestion, they glanced with a shopper's eye at the market stalls, where shallots hung in bouquets, and crisp lettuce, leeks, and celery stalks were placed attractively alongside radishes, beets, carrots, butter beans, "alligator pears" (avocados), and Brussels sprouts. Then came an array of seasonings: thyme and bay leaves, sage and parsley; and everywhere the big silver bells of garlic, braided on their own beards.

Close by the vegetable market and adding their own delightful scents to the mixture of aromas were the flower stalls, where vendors sold daisies and roses, camellias and little bouquets of violets in paper cones. My grandmother often took a bouquet home to use as a centerpiece for Sunday dinner. Italian vendors, who had immigrated to New Orleans in great numbers in the 1890s, had settled in the Quarter and found employment in the French Market.

In the fish market, laid out on gray marble slabs, a variety of fish in shades of gray and pink and silver waited to be purchased. There were latanier baskets of blue-clawed crabs and, in season, crawfish looking like tiny lobsters, and river shrimp still fighting for their lives. Croakers hung in silver bunches, and pompanos lay side by side with bluefish, Spanish mackerel, and trout, ready for tenderloining. If a shopper bought live crabs to boil, the vendor put them in her basket and covered them with a handful of Spanish moss, which got tangled in their claws and stopped them from getting away.

Daddy used to say you could buy anything from the sea in the meat building of the French Market: turtle meat in steaks, turtle eggs, flounders, grouper fish, and even alligator meat. Over furnaces standing on tripods, women cooked fried oysters and fish, as well as ham and eggs for those who chose to have their breakfast or brunch at the market instead of cooking at home.

And there was always coffee, almost at every stall, its aroma drawing Orleanians like a drug. *Café au lait* hit the spot, or sometimes *café noir,* if you were in the mood for a strong wake-me-up.

THE PUBLIC MARKET CONCEPT SPREAD

By the 1920s, there were more than two dozen public markets operated by the city government. They were an integral part of American town life in many cities, but New Orleans had more than any other city and they survived to a much later date.

The concept of city-operated markets goes back to the city's founding, when the site of the French Market was an Indian trading place. Even before the Civil War, many more markets had been built. City ordinance decreed that these establishments had a monopoly on food distribution, though pushcart peddlers were still allowed to sell their wares.

Among the oldest was St. Mary's Market, built in 1836 on the edge of the Irish Channel. It closed in 1922. Another early market was the Poydras Market (1830), which was two blocks long, set in the neutral ground of Poydras Street between Baronne and Rampart streets. Other early markets were St. Bernard (still operating), Treme (which was located on the neutral ground of Orleans Avenue), Port, Claiborne, Dryades, Magazine, Soraporu, Ninth Street, and Carrollton. Off and on, these markets had a virtual monopoly of food distribution, and citizens had little choice but to patronize them. The last of the city's thirty-four markets was built in 1911, and by that time, many of the older ones were closing because they were charging higher prices, losing patronage, and deteriorating.

In 1920, the State Board of Health issued an injunction against several public markets, claiming that they were unsanitary. By the late twenties, the public market system was in terrible shape. Many people had moved out of the areas of the public markets to newer neighborhoods. A study proved that the city was operating too many markets, that they were filthy, and that price fixing was taking place. Markets had outlived their usefulness, since their original purpose had been to prevent high prices and bad food.

Poydras Street public market, one of a municipal chain of thirty-four markets in the twenties, ran two blocks long in the neutral ground of Poydras from Baronne to Rampart Street. This picture was taken from Poydras and Dryades (looking uptown). (Courtesy The Historic New Orleans Collection, acc. no. 1974.25.20.83)

St. Roch Market, St. Claude Avenue between Marais and Music streets, was built in the nine-teenth century and still operates as a market. When built, it was not enclosed but marked by stalls within an open space. (Photo by Susann Gandolfo)

Fliers were circulated, asking New Orleanians to demand the end of the public market system. Since independent meat dealers were not allowed to operate in most parts of the city, the price of meat in public markets was sky high. Weiners were twenty-five cents a pound in public markets and ten cents a pound in private butcher shops. Poor families either had to buy from public markets or walk miles to private markets to get the same food at half the price.

Throughout the twenties, the city was accused of spending the revenues of public markets on political jobs, while ordinary citizens suffered. People were reticent, however, to give up the public markets, for fear that Northern-owned chain stores would take them over. In the twenties, three markets were closed down, but nine were rebuilt and eleven others renovated.

HELP FOR THE MARKETS CAME TOO LATE

By the thirties, New Orleanians were disenchanted with public markets, and although WPA funds became available to help clean them up, the help had come too late. New Orleanians were changing their shopping habits. Small independent neighborhood grocery stores and meat markets were springing up on almost every corner. The city began leasing its public market buildings to private concerns. Some market buildings were leased to other kinds of businesses, like firehouses (Delamore Market) and rug dealers (Suburban Market).

By the time my mother and father were married in 1924, and moved to Orleans Street near City Park in 1927, there was a small grocery on one corner of the back street (St. Peter Street) and a drugstore on the other. The neighborhood meat market was two doors away. All were in close walking distance. No one complained about commercial enterprises in residential neighborhoods. They could not have lived without them. Shopping was done daily, and most housewives did not drive cars.

Much fresh produce was also bought from vendors, who plied their trade in mule-drawn wagons on the narrow rutted streets of the city, singing out the kind of merchandise they had to offer to the tune of their own made-up melodies. Their produce was always fresh, and bargaining was one of the perks of the transaction.

The main dining room of the Grunewald Hotel (later the Roosevelt, now the Fairmont), at 123 Baronne Street. Built in 1893, the hotel was refurbished in 1923 and renamed the Roosevelt.

CHAPTER SIXTEEN

Hotels, Clubs, and Restaurants

I'll be down to get'cha in a taxi, honey,
You better be ready by a half past eight.
Now honey don't be late;
I wanna be there when the band starts playin.'

NEW ORLEANS HAS ALWAYS BEEN KNOWN for its fine inns and restaurants. As a port city, it has attracted businessmen; as an historic city, it has been a magnet for tourists. In the mid-nineteenth century, planters came in the fall of the year to transact business and enjoy the opera; in the spring, they came with their families for Mardi Gras.

King and queen of the Proteus Carnival Ball, 1927.

A float in the Rex parade, 1927. Note the sheet-shrouded mules pulling floats, with holes cut out for ears and eyes. Floats carried only four to six maskers.

OUR HISTORIC HOTELS

The Grunewald/Roosevelt, known under first one name, then the other, in the 1920s, is one of the oldest hotels in the city still in operation. It was built by Louis Grunewald in 1893 and renamed for Theodore Roosevelt in 1923. Its entrance is on University Place but it is listed in the telephone directory as 123 Baronne. Its lobby crosses the entire block from University to Baronne. Situated beneath the lobby directly under what is now the recently reopened Blue Room was The Cave, believed to be America's first nightclub. It was decorated with waterfalls, stalactites, and stalagmites.

The hotel's guest rooms were reached by corridors lined with wall sconces trimmed with strings of crystal beads, and its overhead lights were draped with crystal beads hanging like necklaces from the centers to the edges of the circular fixtures. Plush multicolored carpets covered the floors, and the furniture was elegant and costly.

Knight Templars Conclave held its convention in April 1922 at the Grunewald Hotel. This double-arched monument was erected on Canal Street for the event.

The Monteleone, 214 Royal Street, purchased by Antonio Montelone, a cobbler from Contessa, Italy, in 1893, was at the time a fourteen-room hotel called the Commercial Hotel. Rooms were added as the years went by: 30 rooms in the early 1900s, 200 in 1908 when an eleven-story building was completed, and 200 more in 1928. The name was changed to the Monteleone in 1908.

The Monteleone was one of the most elegant hotels of the twenties, with a beautiful lobby, richly carpeted and hung with chandeliers. In the dining room, musicians played stringed music while patrons dined.

One day in 1928, a traveling salesman from the New York Air Conditioning Company called at the Monteleone. "Why don't you let me put air-conditioning in your hotel?" he asked the manager.

"No, thanks," said manager James Kenny. "If we put air-conditioning in, somebody'll catch pneumonia and the customers will be standing in line to sue us."

Corner of the mezzanine of the new Monteleone Hotel at 214 Royal Street, early 1920s. The name changed from Commercial Hotel in 1908 when 200 rooms were added. In 1928, 200 more rooms were added.

The salesman didn't take no for an answer, and four years later, air-conditioning was installed in the first five floors. The customers were standing in line, but not to sue. They were begging for rooms.

The DeSoto Hotel, which originally faced Baronne Street (now Le Pavillon facing Poydras), was once part of the Gravier plantation in the early 1800s. The New Orleans and Carrollton Railroad put a depot on the very spot where the hotel later stood. After the depot was torn down, the site was used for a theater. A succession of uses followed until finally, construction began in 1905 of a new

The main dining room of the DeSoto Hotel on Baronne and Perdido, 1920s. Built as the Denechaud Hotel in 1905, it was sold in 1913 and renamed the DeSoto.

The lounge of the DeSoto Hotel (today Le Pavillon on Poydras). The mural depicts City Park with its Peristyle.

nine-story Denechaud Hotel built in the "modern Renaissance" style. In 1913, it was sold and became the DeSoto Hotel. Only a few of the rooms had private baths in the twenties. Guests used a community bath on each floor.

The facades of the Monteleone and the Roosevelt were of glazed terra-cotta, a style revived at the Chicago Columbian Exhibition in 1893. The facade of the DeSoto was of terra-cotta made to resemble stone. All were designed by the architectural firm of Wogan and Toledano.

The Pontchartrain Hotel was completed in 1927 and was the first apartment hotel in New Orleans. Real-estate developer Albert Aschaffenburg, who had planned to build a hotel called The Pontchartrain on University Place in 1917, died in 1918 at the age of forty-nine. His son, E. Lyle Aschaffenburg, who was returning from World War I, then became president and manager of the Lafayette Hotel. It was he who promoted and raised the money in the 1920s for an "apartment" hotel, the first of its kind in the city, called The Pontchartrain, which was to be located on St. Charles Avenue near the Garden District. Finished in 1927, it was a twelve-story, eighty-unit building. Gradually Mr. Aschaffenburg gained total ownership. He opened the now famous Caribbean Room, which was an immediate success, not only for his hotel guests but for New Orleanians in general.

The Jung Hotel (today the Clarion), at 1500 Canal Street, was billed as "the hotel of smiling service." Opened in 1925 by the Jung family, this ten-story, 323-room hotel had such modern luxuries as baths, air-conditioning, steam heat, and

The Jung Hotel interior (now the Clarion). Opened in 1925, it was acclaimed the "largest and most magnificent hotel in the South." It boasted baths, air-conditioning, steam heat, and ceiling fans. The roof-garden ballroom with a roll-back roof (added three years later) made this the setting for premier events in the area. (Courtesy the Clarion Hotel)

ceiling fans. It featured travertine walls, a handmade tile fountain, tapestry-upholstered chairs, and Turkish baths. The hotel was such an immediate success that three years later, an eighteen-story annex with 375 rooms was added. The annex was topped with an "All Year Roof," a roof garden that had the flexibility of a roll-back roof with disappearing windows that changed the ceiling into a blanket of stars. Here, the premier events of the city took place, from elaborate balls to high school proms.

This "skyscraper" was built in an eclectic, historical style, using sculptural details to accent simple facades with a combination of Renaissance and baroque elements. It represented the taste of the time prior to the modernist movement.

The St. Charles Hotel no longer exists, but in the twenties, it stood at 211 St. Charles Avenue in the curve of the street where its majestic facade was visible from Canal Street. It occupied that location for a total of 130 years. Fires razed the first two St. Charles hotels. Most New Orleanians remember the third and

The St. Charles Hotel (the third built on the same site after the first two were razed by fire), at 211 St. Charles Avenue, was visible from Canal Street, standing in the curve of the avenue. Today it is the site of the Place St. Charles.

The opulent two-story lobby of the St. Charles Hotel, 1924.

191

last St. Charles Hotel, which opened in 1896. It was a large Romanesque structure with a grand, two-story lobby in which a magnificent staircase led to a surrounding balcony. For sixty years, it was the scene of Mardi Gras balls and debutante parties. At that site today stands the Place St. Charles.

NEW ORLEANS CLUBS OF THE TWENTIES

The Southern Yacht Club is the second oldest in the country, following the New York Yacht Club by five years. A yacht club building for members was not constructed right away, but boating action began as early as 1849 with a regatta in which eighteen boats contended for the championship. In the beginning, headquarters for the winter months was the Verandah Hotel in New Orleans.

The opening of the first clubhouse was celebrated June 5, 1879. It was a one-story frame structure. A later clubhouse opened May 7, 1921, an elegant building with polished hardwood floors, the largest dance floor in the city, a well-appointed dormitory, and a ladies' lounge furnished in ivory wicker. This was the club enjoyed by New Orleanians in the twenties.

The Southern Yacht Club team tied with the Pensacola Club for first place in the Labor Day Sir Thomas J. Lipton Cup Regatta. In 1925, the SYC team won all alone.

In the foyer of the Southern Yacht Club, three "one-arm bandits" and an "iron claw" machine provided amusement for the members until the law intervened and banned gambling in the Parish of Orleans. Since the clubhouse was on the borderline of Jefferson Parish, where gambling was permitted, the SYC claimed residence in Jefferson for as long as it was possible.

The New Orleans Country Club was built in 1914 on the Old Shell Road and the New Basin Canal (the present-day Pontchartrain Expressway) on land that

The New Orleans Country Club was moved in 1914 to the Old Shell Road. It is the oldest country club in the area.

was originally the Oakland Park tract. It was the "highest undivided tract available," according to the prospectus, and it was shaded by many beautiful oaks. Its location made it accessible to motorists, boatsmen, and the streetcars of Carrollton Avenue and Canal Street. The clubhouse burned down in 1921 and was rebuilt the following year. Fortunately a 300-year-old oak survived the fire and offers a picturesque view from the Founders' Room.

The club's interior was designed by Charles Gresham. Its facilities included an eighteen-hole golf course, twelve tennis courts, a swimming pool, a pro shop, and full dining and entertainment areas.

Many confuse the New Orleans Country Club with the earlier and distinctly separate Country Club of New Orleans (1903-17), which was located in City Park, facing Bayou St. John. This older club burned down in 1917 and was not rebuilt. There was no corporate connection between the two (though many citizens were members of both clubs). (Today's Vista Shores Club used the design of the Country Club of New Orleans.)

Metairie Country Club was situated off Airline Highway just over the parish line on Metairie Ridge. In the twenties, it was only a golf club. In 1925, the golf course was completed. It had been designed by a golf-links architect with each hole a replica of a celebrated hole in some golf course in the United States or Scotland. Metairie did not become a full-fledged country club until 1945.

The Boston Club, at 824 Canal Street, founded in 1841, occupied the Mercer House in 1884 and bought the building in 1905. It is the third oldest men's club in America (after Philadelphia Club and Union Club in New York). It was named, not after Boston, Massachusetts, but after a popular card game of the time. It has no Carnival affiliation, but many members of the Boston Club are also members of the Mystick Krewe of Comus. In the twenties, the Rex organization queen and court sat in the Boston Club stands on Mardi Gras day, and Rex himself was traditionally a member of the Boston Club. It was always an all-male club. The Boston Club is a landmark, and it has always been painted white.

The Pickwick Club, at 115 St. Charles Avenue, was founded in 1857 by members of the Mystick Krewe of Comus, and had a direct affiliation with that organization until 1888. Like the Boston Club, it was an all-male club.

The Louisiana Club, at 707 Union Street, was founded in 1872. All members were also members of the Knights of Momus Carnival Organization. It, too, was an all-male club.

The Stratford Club, at 818 Gravier Street, was founded in 1897. All members were also members of the Mithras Carnival Organization.

The West End Country Club was, in the twenties, a leading club with a splendid clubhouse, golf course, and tennis courts on the West End Old Shell Road just beyond Metairie Cemetery, fronting on the New Basin Canal. At this same location, the Lakewood Country Club was founded in 1936. It was begun by a group of Jewish business- and professional men who, for all practical purposes, were barred from the area's old-line clubs. In 1958, the Federal Highway Commission came in with plans to build the I-10 right through the club's back nine. The club sold the property needed to the federal government and the rest of the land to the Livaudais brothers, who subdivided it into the residential area called Lakewood South. The country club building was leased to New Orleans Academy, and has since been demolished. Lakewood Country Club is now located at 4801 General de Gaulle Drive in Algiers.

In the twenties, the West End Country Club faced the Old Shell Road just past the Metairie Cemetery going toward the lake. It was one of the most beautiful of the six New Orleans country clubs, featuring a golf course open all year. (Photo by Charles L. Franck, courtesy Earl K. Long Library, UNO)

The YMCA—Young Men's Christian Association—at 936 St. Charles Street facing Lee Circle, offered a swimming pool, gymnastic equipment, and social and charitable activities.

The Chess, Checkers, and Whist Club met in 1880 to debate the founding of a club with rooms of its own. At that time, there were 52 members. The club grew as it moved from place to place. Finally it took possession of its own quarters on Bourbon Street between Canal and Iberville. In time, its membership was 1,000. It was a purely social club, and it attracted attention with its chess tournaments, which brought to New Orleans many of the most renowned chess players in the world.

The Young Men's Gymnastic Club, at 224 North Rampart, was organized in 1872 but for some years it bore the name of the Independent Gymnastic Club. Inside the building is a marble swimming pool and a splendidly appointed gymnasium.

The Masonic Temple, at the corner of St. Charles and Perdido, laid its foundations in 1891. A Masonic Order had been established in New Orleans as early as 1793. In the Masonic Temple, the order pursued its charitable causes.

The Elks Building was erected on Elks Place, a half-block from the Terminal Station on Canal and Basin streets. A pretty strip of park ran down the neutral ground fronting the building, and in the center of that park stood a bronze elk. In the Elks Building, members of that fraternal order held meetings, planned charities, and presented their annual memorial days.

194

RESTAURANTS IN NEW ORLEANS IN THE TWENTIES

Some of the old French Quarter restaurants, which were doing a brisk business with home folk as well as tourists in the twenties, were Galatoire's at 209 Bourbon Street, Antoine's at 713 St. Louis Street, Arnaud's at 813 Bienville, Broussard's at 819 Conti, and the Louisiane Restaurant at 725 Iberville.

Kolb's Restaurant, at 125 St. Charles Avenue, specialized in German food. They celebrated the *Oktoberfest* annually, and had a German oompah band on weekends and special occasions.

Commander's Palace, at 1403 Washington Avenue, had already gained a reputation for fine food, and Delmonico's, at 1300 St. Charles Avenue, was an "in" place to go for a special dinner. Gluck's had four restaurants in town at the end of the twenties: 206 St. Charles, 1115 Canal, 124 Royal, and 437 St. Charles.

Other well-known specialty restaurants were College Inn at 336 North Rampart, Holland House at 902 City Park Avenue, Manale's at 1838 Napoleon, Mandich's at 1201 North Rampart, and Maylie's on the corner of Poydras and Dryades. Maylie's served one menu to all patrons, and was renowned for its ancient wisteria vine, which covered the front of the building with lavender blossoms.

The Vault Department of the Hibernia Bank, Carondelet and Gravier, 1925.

CHAPTER SEVENTEEN

Buy till You Bust: The Crash of '29

Runnin' wild, lost control,
Runnin' wild, mighty bold, Feelin' gay, restless too . . .

IN 1923, CALVIN COOLIDGE TOOK OFFICE as president when Warren G. Harding died. Coolidge was elected to another four years in office in 1924. The country was under the administration of four presidents in the twenties—Wilson (briefly), Harding, Coolidge, and Hoover. A famous quote of President Coolidge was, "The business of America is business."

When the postwar recession ended, around 1922, people were spending money as never before. Manufacturers were producing more and better things: electric refrigerators, radios, faster cars, and modern bathroom fixtures. President Coolidge's method of keeping all this going was to interfere as little as possible and make as few changes as possible in the system.

Due to mass production, corporations were netting huge sums, much of which they were plowing back into further expansion. In 1923, U.S. Steel reduced the workday of its employees to eight hours, employed 17,000 more workers, and was still able to raise wages and show an increase in profits.

Savings stabilized. Savings and life insurance doubled. And for the first time, the country saw the growth of chain stores and the beginning of installment buying. Prosperity was here, and it seemed to show no sign of leaving.

People used these optimistic signals and the abundance of available credit as good reasons for taking advantage of "get-rich-quick" opportunities. By 1928, the prices of stocks were soaring. Thousands of ordinary citizens who had never bought stocks in their lives braved the fearsome stock market, seeking a share of the "instant profits." The success of a number of stock-market "players" encouraged many to believe that business would continue to prosper and expand. It seemed almost unpatriotic not to buy things.

Economist Roger Babson warned, "Sooner or later, a crash is coming, and it may be terrific." But no one was listening. Optimism had become a way of life.

Carondelet Street was the Wall Street of New Orleans. The large building is the American Bank.

197

Hibernia Bank, 1925. Its height, including the tower surmounting its twenty-three floors, went unsurpassed for about two generations. This interior photo was of the Savings Department.

If it hadn't been for those "small down payments and easy monthly payments," most Americans who bought cars in the twenties would have continued to travel horse-and-buggy style. But "Pay as you go" became a slogan to live by, and it soon applied not only to cars, but to vacuum cleaners, refrigerators, radios, and furniture. The question was: how much credit buying could the individual and the country stand?

Some still considered it a virtue to live within one's means. Installment buying added 11 to 40 percent to the cost of an article. Therefore, the buyer was mortgaging his future earnings to gratify his present wants. On the other hand, some modern economists considered credit buying a part of the new prosperity. If a man bought on credit and paid his bills, he established a "good credit rating," a new term in the twenties.

If a piano cost $445, you could have it in your home for $15 down and $12 a month. A sofa priced at $74.50 could be had for $5 down and $8 a month, and a refrigerator was comparable. Why not enjoy these things while paying on them?

The "easy payment" system spawned many a joke. One went like this: "I just paid the doctor another ten dollars on his bill," said the husband. To which the wife replied, "Oh, good. Two more payments and the baby will be ours."

THE CHAIN CONCEPT

Networks of chain stores were spreading across the country. Such chains as Bohacks (groceries), Childs (restaurants), United Drugs, Lerner's (ladies' clothing), Esso stations, and Fanny Farmer Candy Stores were able to cut costs through volume purchasing, and pass on the savings to the consumer. A & P Stores bought a half-billion dozen eggs a year, and could afford to set its prices several cents lower per dozen than the corner grocery store. Piggly-Wiggly was the first grocery chain to have self-service, where the customer followed a traffic pattern and selected his own merchandise, thus cutting labor costs.

Another example of "chaining" was taking place in the lucrative movie industry. Tickets cost as little as ten cents in some theaters and never more than seventy-five cents in others. Admissions in the theaters by 1922 were spiraling up to forty million, and that figure doubled by the end of the decade.

When the movie industry was new, there were three entities involved: producers, distributors, and theater owners, each a separate interest. But moviemakers, who had the product and therefore the upper hand, were able to take over many of their distributors. They also bought up theaters, to shut out rivals' films and make more money showing their own. By 1927, almost all the nation's theaters and distributors had been bought up by producers and were assembled into a few chains. In New Orleans, there were theaters owned by the Saenger Amusement Company, the Orpheum Circuit, and the Loew's Chain.

The industry continued to grow, and movie palaces went up, lavish buildings where theatergoers enjoyed the ambience as much as the movie.

COLLAPSE OF THE MARKET

The straw that broke the camel's back on the stock market and signaled the end of prosperity in the Coolidge administration was the practice of "buying on margin." In the summer of 1929, stocks were not only priced far above their real value, but could be purchased for a marginal down payment of only 10 percent, with the rest of the price financed by brokers' loans.

As stock prices began to slump, investors were required to put up additional margin. Many could get the money only by selling off shares at low prices. This drove the market down swiftly, and caused brokers to again demand more margin. Between October and November, stocks lost more than 40 percent of their valuation, or $30 billion in paper values. In those few weeks, the floor of the New York Stock Exchange was a scene of bedlam.

On Black Tuesday, October 29, 1929, stocks suffered their worst losses. In New Orleans, the *States* evening newspaper ran this story:

STOCK ORGIES HIT BUILDER, FARMER, SAY BANKERS
MORTGAGE MEN SEEK WAY TO AVOID SLUMP DUE TO SPECULATION

Stock prices again crashed disastrously this forenoon, hundreds of issues reaching new lows for the year, and many selling for 1/4 to 1/2 of their high levels of a few weeks ago. Large scale banking support was immediately organized, J.P. Morgan & Co., the National City Bank, Guaranty Trust, and other leading institutions reducing their margin requirements for demand loans from about 40 to 20 percent, thereby releasing an enormous amount of credit to support the market.

Tales of suicide became the talk of the day. Even New Orleans Pelicans president "Heine" Heinemann took his own life in the clutches of depression and guilt for having encouraged his friends to play the market, thereby losing large amounts of money. Thousands of people lost everything but their lives.

President Hoover told the people, "The fundamental business of the country, that is, production and distribution of commodities, is on a sound and prosperous basis." However, certain conditions said otherwise. Banks and corporations were structurally weak and, in some cases, undermined by fraud. Ninety percent of the nation's wealth was in the hands of 13 percent of the people, while the large segments of society—farmers, coal miners, and textile workers—had hardly enough income to meet their minimal needs. The stock-market crash was not only a punishment to greedy speculators; it was a warning to everyone.

Economists insisted that prospects were bright, and everyone wanted to believe them. People resumed their business pursuits, and they kept on spending, but prosperity was not just around the corner. It was gone and would not be back for a very long time.

In New Orleans, however, many great strides had been made in the twenties that would make everyday life easier and more comfortable for everyone in the years to come.

The Industrial Canal (the Inner Harbor Navigation Canal), connecting the river to the lake, was opened at a cost of $20 million. The Five-Mile Bridge over Lake Pontchartrain was completed. Natural gas was brought into New Orleans and made available to homes, businesses, and factories at greatly reduced rates.

The *Morning Tribune* made its bow in the newspaper field. Airmail lines were started and were in full operation. The public school authorities built fifteen new buildings. Seven new hotels were built and extensive improvements and additions were made to others.

The $27-million Lake Pontchartrain improvement project was well under way. City Park tripled in size at a cost of $2 million. The new Municipal Auditorium (costing $2 million) and the new Criminal Court and Prison (also costing $2 million) were well under way toward completion.

Modern disposal of garbage by incineration was provided. The population grew
to an estimated 437,000. The miles of paved streets increased from 187 to almost
300 miles.

New Orleans was in great shape as the decade closed. This was fortunate, since
the Great Depression and World War II would make additional improvements im-
possible for the next fifteen years.

New Orleans City Hall on St. Charles Avenue facing Lafayette Square, built in 1850 by James Gallier. City Hall was moved to Loyola Avenue in the 1950s.

Index

INDEX

Murray, Rai Graner, 145
Olmsted Brothers, 143
Pizatti Gate (City Park), 142
Popp Fountain, 143
Rieker, Albert, 145
Wilson, Samuel, 143
Sewerage and Water Board, 25, 40,
42, 43
Shaw, Archbishop John W., 51
Shushan Airport, 113, 144
Steam pleasure boats
Camellia, 70
Capitol, 151
J.S., 151
President, 150
Southdown, 70
Susquehanna, 70
Sydney, 150
Stores
Adler's, 177
Feibleman's, 169
Godchaux, 173, 176
Holmes, D. H., 144, 173, 174,
176
Krauss, 104, 173, 177
Kress, 85, 177
Maison Blanche, 90, 173-74, 177
Rougelot's, 169
Werlein's, 89, 177
Woolworth's, 171
Storyville, 20, 147
Streetcars, 102

Theaters
Alamo, 76
Athenaeum, 84
Crescent, 76

Famous, 79
Globe, 77
Liberty, 79
Loew's Crescent, 75
Loew's State, 81, 83, 84, 85
Lyric, 78
Orpheum, 79, 81, 83
Palace, 78
Plaza, 85
Poche, 79
Saenger, 57, 81, 83, 85, 90, 104
Saenger St. Charles, 79
St. Charles, 79
St. Charles Orpheum, 79
Star, 77
Strand, 61, 76-77, 85
Trianon, 77
Tudor, 77, 83, 84
Tulane, 75, 76
Thomas, Perley A., 102

Uhalt, Joseph, 89
Uhalt, William, 89
University area, 23

Vieux Carré Commission, 135

WPA Writers' Project, 154
Walmsley, T. Semmes, 57
Wedell, James R., 111
Wedell-Williams Air Service Inc., 111
Weiss, Dr. Carl A., 61
"White Wings," 43
Widmer Electric Company, 44
Williams, Harry P., 111
Wood, A. Baldwin, 25
Wood Pump, 25